CW01640777

Friedrich Dürrei

Der Besuch der alten Dame

Sydney G. Donald

Senior Lecturer in German
University of Leeds

UNIVERSITY OF GLASGOW
FRENCH AND GERMAN PUBLICATIONS
1999

University of Glasgow French and German Publications

Series Editors: Mark G. Ward (German)
Geoff Woollen (French)

Consultant Editors: Colin Smethurst
Kenneth Varty

Modern Languages Building, University of Glasgow,
Glasgow G12 8QL, Scotland

First published 1990.
Revised edition 1993; reprinted 1999.

© Copyright UNIVERSITY OF GLASGOW FRENCH & GERMAN PUBLICATIONS.

All rights reserved. No part of this publication may be reproduced, stored in a retrieval system, or transmitted, in any form or by any means, electronical, mechanical, recording or otherwise, without the prior permission of the publisher.

Printed by University of Glasgow Printing Department.

ISBN 0 85261 342 3

Contents

Introduction

The Swiss playwright Friedrich Dürrenmatt was born on 5th January, 1921 in the Bernese village of Konolfingen, where his father was the Protestant minister. In 1935 the family moved to Bern. After five years of inconclusive studies first at Zürich University then at Bern, Dürrenmatt moved to Basel for a time, then to Ligerz, a village on the Bieler See, before settling down in 1952 with his wife and young family in a house perched high above the French-speaking city of Neuchâtel, where he continued to live until his death on 14th December, 1990.

Dürrenmatt began writing short stories intended for publication about 1943. His first play to be performed, a bawdy, blasphemous piece entitled *Es steht geschrieben*, was given its première at the *Schauspielhaus*, Zürich on 19th April, 1945, and enjoyed an immediate *succès de scandale*. Dürrenmatt's third play, *Romulus der Grosse*, appeared in 1949 and established his name in Europe, and *Der Besuch der alten Dame*, his sixth, confirmed him once and for all as a world-class dramatist. Completed in 1955 and first performed in Zürich on 29th January, 1956, it has since played to enthusiastic theatre-audiences from an enormous range of cultural and political backgrounds throughout the world. It has also been filmed and scored as an opera. Although *Der Besuch der alten Dame* was written with the Western Europe of the booming fifties in mind, it has also provided spectators in virtually every corner of the globe with entertainment and food for thought, and it continues to do so amid the affluence of the last decades of the century.

The stage history of *Der Besuch der alten Dame* is one of almost unqualified success, east and west, in capitalist and communist countries alike. The play owes its remarkable impact first and foremost to the fact that it maps, uncannily, unerringly, but also entirely unsanctimoniously, one of the ugliest and most notable features of life in the latter part of the twentieth century: greed for easy money.

As is so often the case in a work of excellence, the idea behind *Der Besuch der alten Dame* is disarmingly simple. Local girl Kläri Wäscher has made good in the big wide world and is now returning to her home town of Güllen after an absence of many years. Naturally enough, the townspeople are excited about her visit, and when we first see them they are busily preparing to welcome her. Since things have been going rather badly for Güllen lately, and Kläri (who since leaving Güllen has adopted the rather more sophisticated name of Claire) is now the richest woman in the world, her former fellow-citizens are hoping, not unreasonably, that she will help them out of their difficulties with a cash injection. At a banquet in her honour, Claire declares her willingness to contribute 'eine Milliarde' to Güllen–not, as they had hoped, by way of a straight gift, but in the form of an offer they cannot refuse, even though at first they think they can. In short, Claire wants the people of Güllen to kill one of their number, Alfred Ill, the local grocer, Claire's former sweetheart, a popular man and indeed destined to be the next Mayor. To begin with, of course, the townspeople refuse point-blank, but Claire is prepared to wait, and human nature being what it is, it is not long before they have manoeuvred themselves into a position from which the only way to extricate themselves is by delivering the goods in the form of Ill's corpse. Which they do. Whereupon Claire, an incurable romantic in her way, loads the body of the only man she has ever loved into a coffin she has thoughtfully brought along with her, and makes off for the Isle of Capri, where she has a mausoleum with a magnificent view all ready and waiting for Ill who in life, poor man, has barely set foot beyond Güllen.

Chapter One

An Analysis of the Play

The *dramatis personae*

With Dürrenmatt, master of suspense, even something as apparently innocuous as the title of a play or a list of characters is exploited to the full. The biblical-sounding title of his first piece, *Es steht geschrieben*, so misled the theatre-going public of Zürich into thinking that this clergyman's son's writing would be devotional in character that the première nearly ended in a riot when it emerged that the play was actually rather vulgar and irreverent in tone. Similarly, we might be excused for expecting that in the case of *Der Besuch der alten Dame* the eponymous old lady will be a sweet, frail creature, particularly in view of what we learn from the Gülleners in the opening scene about her generosity towards the towns she has visited so far on her tour.

When we go to the theatre, or sit down to read a play, we usually spend the first few moments considering the *dramatis personae* listed in the programme, in order to assimilate the names of the characters and perhaps deduce what we can about their relationships to one another before the curtain goes up. Since suspense is often a major element in a dramatist's repertoire, he may well want to give as little as possible away at this stage, but even so, a look at how an author has *formally* arranged his characters can be instructive.

In *Der Besuch der alten Dame*, Dürrenmatt breaks with the pattern of his previous plays by assigning them to four distinct groups, two major and two minor: *Die Besucher* (Claire Zachanassian and her entourage; *Die Besuchten* (the people of Güllen); *Die Sonstigen* (three railway employees and the bailiff who makes a brief appearance early in Act One); and *Die Lästigen* (two gentlemen of the Press in Act Two plus a radio reporter and a camera man in Act Three).

Among 'The Visited' (we do not yet grasp the significance of Dürrenmatt's use of the passive voice), no one apart from Ill is graced with a name. Instead, the townspeople are referred to in the list of *dramatis personae* either by their relationship to Ill ('Seine Frau', 'Sein Sohn'); by their profession ('Der Bürgermeister', 'Der Polizist');

or simply as ciphers ('Der Erste Bürger', 'Zweite Frau', etc.). A closer inspection of the list of 'Visitors' reveals that something of the sort is true of the characters in this category too: they also include generic names like 'The Butler' and 'Her Husbands VII-IX'; and even if the remainder of her retinue appear to have individual names, that individuality is at once made questionable by their similarity of sound: Toby, Roby, etc.

In fact, it soon becomes obvious that there are only two 'real' characters in *Der Besuch der alten Dame*: Claire and Ill. Claire's entourage consists at any given moment of one husband who is so dispensable, so interchangeable that, as the stage-directions tell us, Husbands VII, VIII and IX can all be played by the same actor (58, 113).

All of the other characters are *either* de-humanised, as we shall learn in the course of the play, by virtue of their association with and dependence on Claire, *or* they are type-cast and identified solely by their profession or function. In fact, this apparently stylised dramatic treatment of the various inhabitants of Güllen actually reflects the reality of small-town or village life, where one is identified within the community, and slotted into the social scheme of things, by one's profession or one's trade; thus the Welsh distinguish between, say, Jones the Butcher, Jones the Blacksmith and Jones the Post. It was a reality well known to Dürrenmatt from his early life in a village:

> [Man lebt] in einer hierarchisch gestuften Welt. Besonders im Dorf. Es typisiert die Menschen. Es ist überschaubar, die Funktion eines jeden ist bekannt, er ist eins mit seiner Funktion: der Gemeindepräsident, der Pfarrer, der Arzt, der Lehrer usw.[1]

As we shall discover, the Clergyman, the Doctor and the Teacher are very important figures, in Güllen as in any small community: they are the three intellectuals, possibly the only three to have had more than an elementary education. As such, in the play, they will become the spokesmen when the time comes to make representations to Claire; and they also, as educated people, act as carriers of the humanistic tradition in the face of threatened barbarity.

---

1 Dürrenmatt, *Stoffe I-III* (Zürich, 1981), 206.

Erster Akt: The exposition and first climax

Welcome to Güllen, a small town 'somewhere in Central Europe'

The scene, when the curtain goes up, is a rather unexpected one: a run-down station platform. Everything shrieks neglect, from the rusty signal-box and the tattered timetable on the wall to the distant view of a dreary street leading off into the town. To one side of the platform there is a small building, its two entrances labelled 'Men' and 'Women'. On a bench in front of this public convenience, sweltering in the sun, sit four men. Nearby, a fifth man, 'indescribably scruffy' (13), is busy inscribing a poster in red with the words 'Willkommen Kläri.' The men's desultory conversation is punctuated at intervals by the roar of express trains thundering by at full tilt, and four heads turn in unison each time to mark the trains' passing. The men know the names of all the expresses and, since they obviously have little else with which to occupy themselves, their times as well:

> DER ERSTE: Die 'Gudrun', Hamburg-Neapel.
> DER ZWEITE: Um elfuhrsiebenundzwanzig kommt der 'Rasende Roland', Venedig-Stockholm.
> DER DRITTE: Das einzige Vergnügen, das wir noch haben: Zügen nachschauen.

It soon transpires that until just five years ago all the express trains, with their exotic-sounding names and exciting destinations, were in the habit of calling at Güllen, but nowadays even the local trains hardly ever stop there.

In the semi-autobiographical *Stoffe I-III*, Dürrenmatt describes how, as a boy, he too used to sit on the platform in Konolfingen, watching the trains and day-dreaming; and he explains how important it was for the self-esteem of a village to be able to boast a fully-fledged 'Bahnhof' at which the expresses called:

> Der Bahnhof [in Konolfingen] hatte das Recht, sich Bahnhof zu nennen–und nicht bloß Station, wie sich die Bahnhöfe in den anderen Dörfern ringsherum eigentlich hätten nennen müssen–, weil er ein Eisenbahnknotenpunkt war, und wir vom Dorf waren stolz darauf: Nur wenige Züge hatten den Mut, nicht anzuhalten, brausten vorbei nach dem fernen Luzern, nach dem näheren Bern. Auf einer Bank vor dem Bahnhof sitzend, sah ich ihnen mit einer Mischung von Sehnsucht und Abscheu entgegen, dann dampften die Lokomotiven, urweltliche Kolosse, vorüber und davon, hinter ihnen, durch die Scheiben der

> Wagenfenster sichtbar, Reisende, die nicht einmal den Bahnhof bemerkten, an welchem sie vorüberschoßen. (*Stoffe I-III*, 16f.)

So the fact that the trains no longer stop at Güllen is far from trivial: it is to be taken as a mark of the town's economic decline; and we also learn that the two major industrial concerns on which the citizens' livelihood has depended, the *Wagnerwerke* and the amusingly named *Platz-an-der-Sonne-Hütte*, have both closed down. Now, it seems, the Gülleners live from hand to mouth, dependent on unemployment benefit and soup kitchens.

As the exposition proceeds, we discover that the disaster which has overtaken Güllen of late is doubly hard to bear, on account of the town's former glory:

> DER DRITTE: Dabei waren wir eine Kulturstadt.
> DER ZWEITE: Eine der ersten im Lande.
> DER ERSTE: In Europa.
> DER VIERTE: Goethe hat hier übernachtet. Im Gasthof zum Goldenen Apostel.
> DER DRITTE: Brahms ein Quartett komponiert....
> DER ZWEITE: Berthold Schwarz das Pulver erfunden.
> DER MALER: Und ich habe mit Glanz die Ecole des Beaux-Arts besucht, doch was treibe ich jetzt? Inschriftenmalerei. (14f.)

The audience is given no time to question how a one-night stopover by Goethe can be sufficient to make Güllen into a 'Kulturstadt', or to wonder how the invention of gunpowder has managed to find its way into a catalogue of cultural achievements; for the conversation immediately turns back to the present, and the first mention of Güllen's expected visitor, 'the billionairess'. The old lady's reputation has gone before her, for she has already shown exceptional generosity in the neighbouring towns of Kalberstadt and Kaffigen, as befits someone who owns, among other things, Armenian Oil, the Northern Broadcasting Company and–a shade incongruously perhaps?–'the 'amusement district' of Bangkok (15). It is high time she came to Güllen, says one of the men, and at that moment, just to emphasise the urgency of the matter, the bailiff arrives aboard the train from Kaffigen. His task, he announces with heavy irony, is a tremendous one, commensurate with the extent of Güllen's plight: 'Pfänden Sie mal eine ganze Stadt' (16)!

The newly-arrived Mayor retorts wryly that there is nothing left worth impounding in Güllen. The town is utterly bankrupt, an astounding state of affairs when one considers that everywhere else prosperity reigns: 'Das Land floriert, und ausgerechnet Güllen ... geht bankrott.' In small-town fashion, the four men on the platform each have their own theories–or rather, their prejudices–about the cause of this 'economic riddle': Güllen has fallen victim, thinks one, to the machinations of the Freemasons; or of the Jews, suggests another; or high finance, speculates the third man; or international communism, according to the fourth. Such mindless remarks, not seriously intended to be malicious in themselves, occur readily to a community which has been struck by dire circumstances for which there is no apparent explanation. In *Stoffe I-III*, Dürrenmatt describes the mixture of puzzlement and unconscious bigotry he witnessed as a boy among the adults of his village as the momentous events of the 1920s and '30s unfolded before their eyes:

> Sie lehnten den Sozialismus ab, weil er nicht aus dem christlichen Glauben entstanden war.... Sie waren nicht Antisemiten, aber die Juden hatten Christus ans Kreuz geschlagen und mußten nun dafür büßen.... Sie standen fassungslos vor dem gewaltigen Geschehen, das die Welt veränderte.... Sie waren stark im Glauben,... und ahnten nicht, wie ohnmächtig sie waren, verwurstelt in eine verlotterte Weltwirtschaft, Spielbälle von politischen Glücksrittern und Hasardeuren der Hochfinanz, Opfer gigantischer Schiebungen und Fehlplanungen. (*Stoffe I-III*, 204)

Like the young Fritz Dürrenmatt, the Gülleners now sit on their station platform and watch the world go by. The passengers behind the carriage windows do not even notice the station they are passing through, and in their narrow isolation the men on the bench have no real inkling of what is going on outside. The station is the point at which the two worlds, the world of Güllen and the world beyond, physically and fleetingly coincide, but they do not in any meaningful sense meet.

Today, however, is different, for today Claire Zachanassian, the most famous citizen of Güllen, and now the richest woman in the world, is coming to visit her home town. She is Güllen's only hope–'Außer Gott. Aber der zahlt nicht' (18)–and frantic preparations are in hand. The Mayor and his fellow-dignitaries, the Teacher and the Clergyman, plan to lay on a civic reception, as banal as their parochial imagination can devise and as elaborate as Güllen's meagre finances can stand. When she arrives on the 1.13 local train from Kalberstadt, she is to be greeted by the tolling of the municipal fire bell (the only one which has not yet been pawned); the mixed choir will sing a folk-song, the town band will play in the market square and the gymnastics club will form a pyramid in her honour. In the evening, there is to be a dinner in the Golden Apostle, though unfortunately the funds will not stretch to illuminating the cathedral and the town hall.

But the fact that their guest has not set foot in Güllen for (as we later discover) some forty-five years is presenting the organisers of the welcoming party with certain difficulties. The once humble Kläri Wäscher is now the celebrated Claire Zachanassian, and although no doubt the Güllener follow avidly her activities, as reported in the world press, and perhaps even derive vicarious pleasure and consolation for their own dreary existences from what they read about her glossy way of life, they actually know very little about her. Their lack of real knowledge and the absence of a coherent plan first begin to emerge in the argument which now develops about the wording of the placard: when 'Willkommen Kläri' is criticised for being 'zu intim', the Painter decides to hedge his bets by writing 'Willkommen Claire Zachanassian' on the reverse and waiting to see how she reacts when she arrives back in her native town: 'Wenn die Milliardärin dann gerührt ist, können wir ihr immer noch die Vorderseite zudrehen' (17).

The townspeople still believe themselves to have a special relationship with Claire, founded on the fact that she is a Güllener born and bred; and the task of the Mayor, as leader of the welcoming party and in the best interests of the town, is to revive and foster that relationship in every way possible. Or, in the cynical terms more appropriate to the workings of the Mayor's mind, Claire has to be made to part with her millions: 'Die Zachanassian soll mit ihren Millionen herausrücken' (19). To this end the Mayor enlists the aid of the town's grocer, Alfred Ill. As Claire's former sweetheart, Ill is not only the acknowledged expert on particulars of Claire's early life, but uniquely equipped to tug at her heart-strings–and hence her purse-strings.

With the help of the Teacher, who has checked back through the records, and Ill and the other bystanders, who have consulted their memories, the Mayor hastily assembles a picture of young Klara. It is not entirely flattering, and will require some retouching by the Mayor in his speech:

> DER LEHRER: Die Noten der Klara Wäscher sind leider, leider herzlich schlecht. Auch das Betragen. Nur in der Pflanzen- und Tierkunde genügend.
> DER BÜRGERMEISTER *notierend*: Gut. Genügend in der Pflanzen- und Tierkunde. Das ist gut.
> ILL: Da kann ich dem Bürgermeister dienen. Klara liebte die Gerechtigkeit. Ausgesprochen. Einmal wurde ein Vagabund abgeführt. Sie bewarf den Polizisten mit Steinen.
> DER BÜRGERMEISTER: Gerechtigkeitsliebe. Nicht schlecht. Wirkt immer. Aber die Geschichte mit dem Polizisten unterschlagen wir besser.

> ILL: Wohltätig war sie auch. Was sie besaß, verteilte sie, stahl Kartoffeln für eine arme Witwe.
> DER BÜRGERMEISTER: Sinn für Wohltätigkeit. Dies, meine Herren, muß ich unbedingt anbringen. Es ist die Hauptsache. (18f.)

But in a quiet corner, amidst the hive of activity on the station platform, the Clergyman initiates a more earnest discussion by asking Ill: 'Sie sind auseinandergegangen damals. Ich hörte eine unbestimmte Geschichte–haben Sie Ihrem Pfarrer etwas zu gestehen?' (18). Ill's reply, however, is quietly reassuring: his words recall the exquisite romance and excitement of first love, when he was 'ein Kerl' and Klara 'eine verteufelt schöne Hexe', and how the inevitable came to pass: 'Das Leben trennte uns, nur das Leben, wie es eben kommt.' And besides: more important than some vague, long-dead rumour, are Ill's prospects for the future. He has long been the most popular man in Güllen, we gather, and now he is tipped to be the next Mayor. Ill is clearly flattered, and when he abandons the sentimental tone of a few moments earlier and slips into the same slick, insincere idiom as the Mayor, it seems as if he is already trying to demonstrate how well he is equipped for the promised post. For Claire, Ill's former sweetheart, their reunion will surely be a poignant, emotionally charged moment, but for Ill, the citizens' chosen spokesman, it is to be approached merely as a tricky diplomatic negotiation: 'Wir müssen klug vorgehen,' he declares self-importantly, 'psychologisch richtig. Schon ein mißglückter Empfang am Bahnhof kann alles verteufeln' (20).

The Mayor is busily outlining his plan of campaign–top hats, his two grandchildren with bouquets, the choir, etc.–when another express comes thundering by: they have two hours left in which to prepare themselves for the big moment. But with a screeching of brakes, and to the utter amazement of all those present, the express comes to a halt alongside the platform. The unthinkable has happened, or, in the words of the station-master, 'Die Naturgesetze sind aufgehoben' (21).

Enter Claire Zachanassian; and what an entrance! She is 'a sixty-two year-old redhead, with a pearl necklace, huge gold bangles, dressed to kill, grotesque, impossible, yet with a curious gracefulness in spite of it all' (22). In her wake are Boby, her butler (about eighty, with dark glasses), and her Husband Number VII (tall, slim, black moustache, fully tricked out for a fishing expedition). Bringing up the rear is an irate railway guard. Despite Dürrenmatt's throwaway description of Güllen as a small town 'irgendwo in Mitteleuropa' (141), the guard's red cap and red leather satchel are unmistakably Swiss, as is his rage at Claire for her unauthorised interference with his timetable. The punctuality of Swiss trains is legendary, and a knowing laugh is guaranteed from the audience when he protests: 'Die Notbremse zieht man nie in diesem Lande, auch wenn man in Not ist. Die Pünktlichkeit des Fahrplans ist oberstes Prinzip' (22).

But Claire Zachanassian has not become the richest woman in the world by obeying pettyfogging officials, nor does she expect to have to be kept waiting. The 12.40 local train which everybody uses–as the guard tells her indignantly–would have got her to Güllen by 1.13. Claire, however, is not 'everybody', and she simply would not consider chugging through the countryside for half an hour, stopping at every village along the route. She is evidently accustomed to having her own way, and she does not mind paying for it. 'Gib ihm tausend, Boby,' she tells her butler, who seems to be armed with wads of notes; 'und dreitausend für die Stiftung zugunsten der Eisenbahnerwitwen' (23). The fact that no Fund for Railwaymen's Widows exists presents no obstacle: she merely tells the guard to set one up. The sight of such large sums of money brings gasps of awe from the bystanders on the platform, intensified by the way in which Claire dismisses them as trivial amounts:

> ALLE *murmelnd*: Viertausend.
> CLAIRE ZACHANASSIAN: Behalten Sie die Kleinigkeit. (24)

But more impressive still is the guard's change of heart. Having by now discovered the identity of his troublesome passenger, he not only tries to return the money, but even to put his entire train at Claire's disposal whilst she does a spot of sightseeing:

> Wünschen gnädige Frau, daß der 'Rasende Roland' wartet, bis Sie Güllen besichtigt haben? Die Eisenbahndirektion würde dies mit Freuden billigen. Das Münsterportal soll sehenswert sein. Gotisch. Mit dem Jüngsten Gericht. (24)

Claire, however, has no further need of the train. She sends the guard on his way and turns to survey the welcoming party, which is now in complete disarray. Thanking the Mayor for his 'fine speech', which has in fact been completely drowned out by the departing train, she walks across to Ill. They greet one another awkwardly, and for a few moments it seems as if this brash, garishly dressed old woman has a sentimental side after all: her whole life through, she tells him, she has wanted to return to Güllen; Ill retorts that he has never stopped thinking about her; 'es war wunderbar,' she remembers, 'all die Tage, da wir zusammen waren' (25); and Ill's aside to the Teacher, though cynical, seems well-judged: 'Sehen Sie, Herr Lehrer, die habe ich im Sack.' Encouraged by Claire, Ill recalls some of the pet names he used to give her–'mein Wildkätzchen,... mein Zauberhexchen'(26)–and the billionairess purrs with delight.

Getting carried away by his new role as pedlar of nostalgia, Ill starts talking arrant nonsense, but he is brought down to earth with a humiliating jolt when, in response to his silly remark that he is still Claire's 'black panther' of yesteryear, she snaps: 'Unsinn. Du bist fett geworden. Und grau und versoffen.' Unperturbed, Ill continues with his senseless flattery: 'Doch du bist die gleiche geblieben. Zauberhexchen.' Claire's sarcastic reply is a model of that brutal outspokenness which only the very rich can afford:

> Ach was. Auch ich bin alt geworden und fett. Dazu ist mein linkes Bein dahin. Ein Autounfall. Ich fahre nur noch Schnellzüge. Doch die Prothese ist vortrefflich, findest du nicht? *Sie hebt ihren Rock in die Höhe und zeigt ihr linkes Bein.* Läßt sich gut bewegen.

Thoroughly unnerved, Ill breaks into a cold sweat. Perhaps their visitor is going to be less easy prey than they thought.

Claire now introduces her seventh husband, Moby. He owns tobacco plantations and his real name is Pedro, but she prefers Moby because it goes better with Boby, the name of her butler, and her husbands have to fit in with him, because 'den hat man schließlich fürs Leben', whereas husbands, she hints, are only there for a short time. Claire, as we shall learn in the course of the play, collects husbands, rather in the way that other people collect thimbles or Toby jugs. 'Einen Mann,' Claire informs Ill in Act III, 'hält man sich zu Ausstellungszwecken, nicht als Nutzobjekt' (114). All of her husbands look alike, apart from the colour of their hair and moustaches, and indeed the stage-directions in Act II, when Husband Number VIII is introduced, state (58) that he can be played by the same actor as Husband Number VII, as can Husband Number IX later on (113). Although Claire's husbands are physical stereotypes, in certain other respects they appear to be exotic and individual; this impression, however, turns out to be illusory, for they are in fact all merely variations on a theme, and as such they provide Dürrenmatt with opportunities for running gags. Husband Number VII, for instance, ponders to order:

> CLAIRE ZACHANASSIAN: Denk nach, Moby.
> *Gatte VII denkt nach.*
> CLAIRE ZACHANASSIAN: Fester.
> *Gatte VII denkt fester nach.*
> CLAIRE ZACHANASSIAN: Noch fester.
> GATTE VII: Aber ich kann nicht fester nachdenken, Mausi, wirklich nicht.

CLAIRE ZACHANASSIAN: Natürlich kannst du's. Probier's nur.
Gatte VII denkt noch fester nach. (26f.)

Husband Number VIII, by contrast, turns out to be a dimwitted film star–'Gedanken sind nicht deine Stärke' (58)–, whilst Husband Number IX is a Nobel Prizewinner who is at his most endearing in those rare moments when he is *not* thinking. 'Er ist besonders eigenartig, wenn er nicht denkt,' she declares. 'Denk mal nicht, Zoby' (114).

Meanwhile, Claire's reception committee has been collecting itself together after a fashion, and the Teacher announces, in pompous, falsely modest, schoolmasterly vein, that the choir will now render a 'homely folk-song' (28). Claire's caustic, slangy reply to this self-styled 'Liebhaber der edlen Frau Musica' (27)–'Fire away with your homely folk-song'–, coupled with the din from another passing train, completely unnerve the choir, which only serves to make Claire's 'Gut gesungen, Güllener' appear all the more insincere.

The time has come now to introduce the members of the welcoming party: first, curiously, the Policeman, then the Mayor's seven-year old twin grandchildren, complete with obligatory red roses. Once again, the atmosphere of solemnity which the Gülleners are so ineptly trying to create is destroyed by Claire's response: 'I congratulate you on your two brats [*Gören*], Mayor' (29). Nor is the dignity of the occasion helped by the fact that there is only one top hat to go round. It has been passed, surreptitiously, from the Teacher to the Mayor, and now it has reached the Clergyman, who slips it to the Doctor when Claire moves along the line. But the amusing features of this scene are undercut by a series of macabre remarks by Claire. First she asks the Policeman if he sometimes turns a blind eye to things, and when he replies in the affirmative, advises him to start turning two. Next she enquires of the Clergyman whether he is in the habit of comforting the dying and those condemned to death. In answer to his shocked reply, that the death sentence has been abolished in their country, Claire says cryptically: 'Man wird sie vielleicht wieder einführen' (29). Finally, she asks the Doctor if he issues death certificates, and recommends that in future he should certify the cause of death as heart attack.

With that, Claire declares the official reception over. She announces imperiously that whilst her retinue and her luggage (a seemingly endless procession of suitcases) make for the Golden Apostle Hotel, she desires to be taken to visit their old lovers' haunts, the *Petersche Scheune* and the *Konradsweilerwald*, with Ill. Not, however, in the Doctor's 1932 Mercedes (the best car the Gülleners can muster), but in a sedan-chair carried by Roby and Toby, two huge gum-chewing thugs, convicted murderers plucked from the electric chair by Claire at a cost of a million dollars per head to be her bodyguards: 'Seit meinem Unfall bewege ich mich nur per Sänfte' (30). And even the sedan-chair is grandiose, as we are by now coming to expect: 'Die Sänfte stammt aus dem Louvre und ist ein Geschenk des französischen Präsidenten' (31).

But Claire's impact on the Gülleners does not end with her theatrical departure. As she is carried off the platform, the cheers of the townspeople die on their lips at the sight of an elaborate black coffin being borne from the train; and bringing up the rear of her entourage are two fat little old men, Koby and Loby. They talk in unison, and both are blind, but they know they are in Güllen, so they say, by the smell, and they know they are talking to a policeman by his intonation.[2] They express surprise when the Policeman addresses them as 'ihr kleinen dicken Männer': 'Männer,' they chortle. 'Er hält uns für Männer!' (32). Foreigners, the Policeman concludes–and here he evokes a laugh by his use of a well-worn cliché–foreigners have a funny sense of humour; but he has entirely misunderstood the joke, for these are not really men at all. They are eunuchs.

So at last, this long, gripping first scene is over and there is an almost palpable easing of tension in the auditorium. After a curtainless scene change, we find ourselves in the Golden Apostle, a once luxurious, but now seedy, threadbare, smelly hostelry, with peeling plaster and so on. The Mayor, the Clergyman and the Teacher are sitting drinking schnaps and watching Claire's luggage arriving. But there is even more to her circus procession than we thought previously:

> DER BÜRGERMEISTER: Koffer, nichts als Koffer.
> DER PFARRER: Haufenweise. Und vorhin wurde in einem Käfig ein Panther hinaufgeschafft.
> DER BÜRGERMEISTER: Ein wildes schwarzes Tier.
> DER PFARRER: Der Sarg.
> DER BÜRGERMEISTER: Wird in ein Extrazimmer gebracht.

2 The point of the joke is that 'Gülle' means 'cess-pool', 'slurry' or 'liquid manure'. If the name of the town is indicative of its nature, this would explain why Claire Zachanassian never actually sets foot on the streets of Güllen! Dürrenmatt enjoys farmyard humour. The eponymous hero of Romulus der Große is a passionate hen-breeder, and the stage is overrun with hens and littered with egg-shells. In Herkules und der Stall des Augias (1963), the hero sets out on his fifth Labour, the cleansing of the Augean Stables. The city of Augias is buried beneath a centuries-old mountain of dung, the actors wear hip-length waders and the entire set is painted a glistening brown.

> DER LEHRER: Seltsam.
> DER PFARRER: Weltberühmte Damen haben ihre Marotten. (33)

Understatement indeed, but despite her quirky ways, the three conclude, their plan appears to be going well. Clearly, with so much luggage, she must be planning to stay a while, and the Mayor, echoing Ill's words, observes: 'Ill hat sie im Sack. Wildkätzchen, Zauberhexchen hat er sie genannt, Millionen wird er aus ihr schöpfen.'

The newly-arrived Policeman reports on developments. Claire and Ill have revisited the *Petersche Scheune*–'eine rührende Szene' (34)–and now they are on their way to their other former trysting-place, the *Konradsweilerwald*. The three men clink glasses to the prospect of Claire's wealth putting Güllen back on its feet again, and to Ill, the Mayor's successor and Güllen's favourite citizen. Only the Teacher expresses some misgivings, but shrouded in a self-important display of erudition, they pass unnoticed:

> Seit mehr denn zwei Jahrzehnten korrigiere ich die Latein- und Griechischübungen der Güllener Schüler, doch was Gruseln heißt, Bürgermeister, weiß ich erst seit einer Stunde. Schauerlich, wie sie aus dem Zuge stieg, die alte Dame mit ihren schwarzen Gewändern. Kommt mir vor wie eine Parze, wie eine griechische Schicksalsgöttin. Sollte Klotho heißen, nicht Claire, der traut man noch zu, daß sie Lebensfäden spinnt.

Yet had anyone been paying attention, they might just have realised the ominous significance of the Teacher's pronouncement, for according to Greek and Roman mythology the Fates, a trio of goddesses known in Greek as *Moirai* and in Latin as *Parcae* (German *Parzen*), are responsible for human destiny: Lachesis assigns man's lot at birth; Clotho, to whom the Teacher likens Claire, spins the thread of life; and Atropos, wielding a pair of scissors, cuts it at the moment of death. Unfortunately, the Teacher is prone to overkill. His conversation is so peppered with learned allusions that no one takes any notice of them, let alone tries to understand them. The next time he speaks he calls Claire, with her string of marriages, 'eine zweite Lais' (Lais was a famous Greek courtesan); and a moment later he is comparing Claire and Ill to Romeo and Juliet and observing with (as it turns out) telling dramatic irony: 'Zum ersten Male in Güllen fühle ich antike Größe' (35).

As the Mayor and the others drink a toast to Ill, the scene changes again: we are in the *Konradsweilerwald*. Claire arrives in her sedan-chair, accompanied by Ill and the whole of her motley retinue, Husband Number VII included. If Claire's bizarre companions appear jarringly out of place in this sylvan setting, the private property, so to speak, of the former sweethearts and their memories, then we may also detect a certain inappropriateness in Dürrenmatt's depiction of the wood itself. The four Gülleners from the station platform now stand with arms outstretched, acting out the part of trees; they imitate the sounds of a woodpecker and a cuckoo, and leap around pretending to be 'shy deer'. Their stated aim is to create an 'echte deutsche Wurzelwildnis' (36). One of them holds up a cardboard heart 'carved' with the couple's initials, and Claire behaves as though the whole scene were authentic:

> Das Herz mit deinem und meinem Namen, Alfred. Fast verblichen und auseinandergezogen. Der Baum ist gewachsen, sein Stamm, seine Äste dick geworden wie wir selber. *Sie geht zu den anderen Bäumen.* Eine deutsche Baumgruppe.

In *Anmerkung I*, a postscript to *Der Besuch der alten Dame* written for the first published version of the play in 1956, Dürrenmatt explains that his chief concern in this scene was to provide a poetic, as opposed to a realistic setting for the lovers' reunion, and thereby to minimise the audience's discomfiture and amusement at the apparent awkwardness of their meeting:

> Wenn die Güllener Bäume spielen, so nicht aus Surrealismus, sondern um die etwas peinliche Liebesgeschichte, die sich in diesem Wald abspielt, den Annäherungsversuch eines alten Mannes an eine alte Frau nämlich–in einen poetischen Bühnenraum zu stoßen und so erträglich zu machen. (141f.)

That may have been Dürrenmatt's intention, and indeed his position regarding this scene remained entirely constant over the years, despite considerable critical comment; but the text seems to lead us to a different conclusion. The Gülleners' efforts to conjure up a romanticised German forest scene, complete with creeping ivy, toadstools and wild life in the manner of Grimms' *Fairy Tales*, are so blatant and so pointedly hamfisted that they simultaneously and continously ironise themselves; and it may well be that Dürrenmatt simply could not resist poking fun at a piece of German cultural heritage just for the fun of it. Certainly there is evidence of ironical intent in the heavy stress he lays on the Germanness of the setting ('echte deutsche Wurzelwildnis', 'eine deutsche Baumgruppe' (36)); and in the punning similarity between his term 'Wurzelwildnis' (36, repeated 39) and Ludwig Tieck's well-known coinage, 'Waldeinsamkeit', a word which is often said to encapsulate the very spirit of German Romanticism. It is, of course, much harder to enthuse about 'a wilderness of tangled roots' than about 'sylvan solitude'. At any rate, the general effect, *pace* Dürrenmatt, *is* either surrealistic or excessively contrived; and the keynote of the scene, as the Gülleners stage their clumsy charade for their visitor's benefit, and Claire and Ill fatuously pretend not to notice the subterfuge, is one of insincerity.

Encouraged by his own newly-discovered eloquence, and abetted at first by Claire, Ill paints an ever more extravagantly rose-tinted picture of their idyllic lost youth, now recaptured at long last:

> CLAIRE ZACHANASSIAN: Wir liebten uns unter diesen Sträuchern, unter dieser Buche, zwischen Fliegenpilzen im Moos. Ich war siebzehn und du noch nicht zwanzig. Dann hast du Mathilde Blumhard geheiratet mit ihrem Kleinwarenladen...
> ILL: Dir zuliebe habe ich Mathilde Blumhard geheiratet.... Du warst jung und schön. Dir gehörte die Zukunft. Ich wollte dein Glück. Da mußte ich auf das meine verzichten.... Wärest du hier geblieben, wärest du ebenso ruiniert wie ich.... Ein verkrachter Krämer in einem verkrachten Städtchen.... Es ist wie einst, wie wir jung waren und kühn, da wir in den Konradsweilerwald gingen, in den Tagen unserer Liebe.... Kühles Holz und Wind in den Zweigen, ein Rauschen, wie die Brandung des Meeres. Wie einst, alles wie einst.... Wäre doch die Zeit aufgehoben, mein Zauberhexchen. Hätte uns doch das Leben nicht getrennt. (37-9)

But Claire's pretence is short-lived, and very soon she resorts to plain talking. As Ill, warming to his task, waxes increasingly lyrical, Claire's cutting retorts go straight over his head, though they are not lost on the audience: to Ill's sickly sentimental, 'Dir zuliebe habe ich Mathilde Blumhard geheiratet', she replies: 'Sie hatte Geld' (37); to his, 'Dir gehörte die Zukunft', she responds darkly: 'Nun ist die Zukunft gekommen'; and in answer to his doleful outburst, 'Ich lebe in einer Hölle, seit du von mir gegangen bist' (38), she intones menacingly: 'Und ich bin die Hölle geworden.'

Although Claire assures Ill that she does not intend to leave her home town in the lurch, a modified impression of Güllen's prospective benefactor is beginning to emerge in the course of this scene. It has been clear since her arrival at the station that this is no feeble geriatric, and we are fast becoming aware that Ill's mixture of amateurish acting and maudlin self-deception is going to be no match for her brand of brutal honesty, coupled as it is with a macabre sense of humour which seems calculated to inflict the maximum degree of embarrassment on her former sweetheart. Indeed, the discomfort experienced by Ill on the station platform, when she lifted her skirt to show off her artificial leg, now turns to humiliation as, carried away by emotion, he forgets the earlier scene and slaps her on the thigh, only to recoil sharply in pain. 'Das schmerzt,' she says mockingly. 'Du hast auf ein Scharnier meiner Prothese geschlagen' (39). But Ill has not yet learned his lesson, and the audience shrieks with laughter when just a moment later, bending romantically to kiss her cool white hand of yesteryear, he discovers that he has been taken in again:

> ILL: Ich liebe dich doch! *Er küßt ihre rechte Hand.* Dieselbe kühle weiße Hand.
> CLAIRE ZACHANASSIAN: Irrtum. Auch eine Prothese. Elfenbein.
> ILL: *läßt entsetzt ihre Hand fahren.* Klara, ist denn überhaupt alles Prothese an dir! (39f.)

But even as we chuckle at Ill's reaction, we share with him, for a brief moment, his sense of horror at the unseemly prospect of this grotesquely mutilated, patched-up old woman; a horror which irrationally is intensified by the outlandish details of her reply and its sinister echo by the two blind eunuchs as the lights go down:

> CLAIRE ZACHANASSIAN: Fast. Von einem Flugzeugabsturz in Afghanistan. Kroch als einzige aus den Trümmern. Bin nicht umzubringen.
> DIE BEIDEN BLINDEN: Nicht umzubringen, nicht umzubringen. (40)

In the course of this brief scene, then, Dürrenmatt has extended our view of the main characters considerably. We are beginning not only to appreciate more fully the complexity of Claire's personality, but also to grasp the essential difference between the two: that Ill, despite being Güllen's favourite citizen and chosen leader, is weak and inclines towards mushy sentimentality, whereas Claire, with her harsh, vulgar brand of realism, is quite the reverse. In this scene, too, there are signs that the relationship between Ill and Claire will not necessarily evolve as the Gülleners intend: far from being an innocent goose for the plucking, Claire is starting to look more like a cat playing with a mouse.

The final scene of Act I takes place in the Golden Apostle, where all the citizens of Güllen have assembled for a banquet and civic reception in Claire's honour. After the municipal band comes a display of skill from the Gymnast, which provides Claire with an opportunity to crack another of her 'Bonmots': admiring his muscles, she asks him, 'Haben Sie schon jemand erwürgt mit Ihren Kräften?' (41). Ill laughs dutifully, but the Doctor has to admit that jokes like this give him the creeps. After a few scathing remarks to two of her exclassmates, now Frau Ill and the Lady Mayoress respectively, Claire announces that her husband will not be coming to the reception: the divorce is already under way and she will shortly be able to fulfil her childhood dream of getting married (to Husband Number VIII) in Güllen Cathedral.

Meanwhile the festivities proper can commence. The Mayor's speech of welcome is a masterpiece of Dürrenmattian irony. It captures perfectly the politician's hyperbole, his sweeping inaccuracy and his blatant distortion of the facts to suit his own ends. Trying desperately to cover both ends of the spectrum, the servile as well as the intimate, the Mayor addresses Claire incongruously as 'gnädige Frau–unsere Kläri' (43). Her drunkard of a father, remembered only for the toilets he built on the station platform, has been turned into 'der volkstümliche Vater, der beim Bahnhof ein von Fachkreisen und Laien stark besuchtes– ... stark beachtetes Gebäude errichtete.' The young Claire is referred to first as 'blond', then as 'rotgelockt'; and her school work, which the Teacher, it will be recalled, had earlier described as 'leider, leider herzlich schlecht' (18f.), has miraculously become 'exemplary'. But most important of all, the Mayor insists, was Kläri's love of justice and her charitableness. Her many acts of benevolence nowadays, he concludes, have their roots in her generosity of spirit as a young girl, typified by the time when she rescued an old widow in Güllen from starvation by buying potatoes for her with her own hard-earned pocket-money.

Claire's reply, when the applause dies down, is sarcastic, brief and to the point: she is moved by the Gülleners' 'selfless' pleasure at her visit; but actually she was forever being thrashed in school; and she *stole* the potatoes for the widow–'the old bawd'–, not to save her from starving, but for quite a different reason: 'die Kartoffeln ... habe ich gestohlen, gemeinsam mit Ill,... um mit Ill einmal in einem Bett zu liegen, wo es bequemer war als im Konradsweilerwald oder in der Peterschen Scheune' (44). As her contribution to the Gülleners' pleasure at seeing her again, however, she wants them to know straight away that she intends to give them 'a billion', five hundred million of it to the city, the other five hundred million shared out equally among all the families in the town.

Such overwhelming generosity, beyond their wildest dreams, is greeted with a 'deathly silence', followed by tumultuous applause. But there is 'one condition', even if some time elapses before the cheering subsides enough to allow the Mayor to ask what the condition is. Claire's answer seems to be at once explicit and vague: 'Ich will die Bedingung nennen. Ich gebe euch eine Milliarde und kaufe mir dafür die Gerechtigkeit' (45). 'What does she mean?' the Mayor enquires. 'Surely one can't *buy* justice.' Claire's reply is unemphatic but chillingly concise: 'Man kann alles kaufen.'

Her butler, Boby, steps forward and removes his dark glasses. 'Der Oberrichter Hofer,' the Teacher gasps. 'Correct,' Boby replies. Forty-five years ago he was a judge in Güllen, and for the past twenty-five years, ever since she made him an irresistible offer, he has been Claire's butler. Now he will explain the terms of Claire's settlement:

> Wie ihr vernommen habt, bietet Frau Claire Zachanassian eine Milliarde und will dafür Gerechtigkeit. Mit anderen Worten: Frau Claire Zachanassian bietet eine Milliarde, wenn ihr das Unrecht wiedergutmacht, das Frau Zachanassian in Güllen angetan wurde. Herr Ill, darf ich bitten. (46)

Ill stands up and shrugs awkwardly, half scared and half puzzled, with a silly grin on his face. As Boby begins his tale, the years roll back and, to borrow a phrase of Dürrenmatt's from another context, 'die Szene wird zum Tribunal' (*Friedrich Schiller-Rede*, 26: 90). The Golden Apostle has turned into a courtroom, and Ill is the accused.

Boby's story, though harrowing, is simple. In 1910, as Judge Hofer, Boby presided over a paternity suit brought by Klara Wäscher against Alfred Ill and contested by him. Ill called two witnesses, Jakob Hühnlein and Ludwig Sparr, both of whom testified that Klara had also slept with them. Their testimony was false, bought by Ill for a litre of schnaps, but they were believed and Klara lost the case. A year later, she also lost the child. Branded a common whore, she was forced to leave town and actually become one. Financially she went from strength to strength, so that now, as the richest woman in the world, she is at last able to afford what was so cruelly denied her long ago, thus satisfying that passion for justice so unthinkingly commended only a few moments earlier by the Mayor.

With a dramatic flourish, Boby produces two witnesses, the blind eunuchs Koby and Loby: they testify that they are the same men, Jakob Hühnlein and Ludwig Sparr, whom Ill bribed in the paternity case. One had emigrated to Canada, the other to Australia, but to no avail: 'die Dame ließ uns suchen' (48). Having tracked them down, she handed them over to the gangsters, Toby and Roby, who meted out an appropriate punishment: 'Kastriert und geblendet, kastriert und geblendet,' they whimper in unison.

But all of this was a lifetime ago, Ill blurts out. He was young and thoughtless then, but surely such matters lapse after so many years? 'Verjährt, alles verjährt! Eine alte, verrückte Geschichte,' he protests.

Completely ignoring Ill, the judge turned butler brings his exposition of the case to a dramatic climax with a concise interrogation of the plaintiff herself:

> DER BUTLER: Was geschah mit Ihnen?
> CLAIRE ZACHANASSIAN: Ich wurde eine Dirne.
> DER BUTLER: Weshalb?

> CLAIRE ZACHANASSIAN: Das Urteil des Gerichts machte mich dazu.
> DER BUTLER: Und nun wollen Sie Gerechtigkeit, Claire Zachanassian?
> CLAIRE ZACHANASSIAN: Ich kann sie mir leisten. Eine Milliarde für Güllen, wenn jemand Alfred Ill tötet. (49)

Claire's macabre proposition is delivered with an air of total confidence and finality, and greeted with numbed incomprehension by the assembled Gülleners. A 'deathly silence' ensues, broken at last by a cry from Ill's wife, and a half-plaintive, half-indignant appeal from Ill himself: 'Zauberhexchen! Das kannst du doch nicht fordern! Das Leben ging doch längst weiter!'

These words carry a faint echo of one of his remarks on the station platform, when he was being asked by the Clergyman to explain his former relationship with Claire: 'Das Leben trennte uns,' he said then, 'nur das Leben, wie es eben kommt' (18). Ill's evasive reply may have silenced the Clergyman, but not Claire. Blaming events on 'life', as though it were some sort of abstract force over which we have no control, will simply not suffice, especially since 'life', for Ill, has been the consequence of choice, whereas for Claire it has been the result of coercion: 'Du hast dein Leben gewählt,' she reminds him, 'und mich in das meine gezwungen' (49). Her memory is long and accurate, and now the time has come to settle old scores. Earlier, in the *Konradsweilerwald*, Ill rashly wished the clock could be turned back, and now his wish has come true with a vengeance: 'und nun will ich Gerechtigkeit, Gerechtigkeit für eine Milliarde.'

The Mayor rises to his feet, 'pale and dignified'. Naturally, what Frau Zachanassian is proposing is quite unacceptable in a humane, civilised society, and he must formally decline on behalf of Güllen:

> Noch sind wir in Europa, noch sind wir keine Heiden. Ich lehne im Namen der Stadt Güllen das Angebot ab. Im Namen der Menschlichkeit. Lieber bleiben wir arm denn blutbefleckt. (50)

Fine words, reassuring rhetoric, though it will not have escaped the more perceptive members of the audience, as we remarked earlier, that Güllen's cultural heritage, which is now being so solemnly invoked, rests on a rather flimsy foundation: an overnight stay by Goethe, a Brahms quartet and, more dubiously still, the invention of gunpowder. All in all, as Act I finally draws to a close, Claire's quietly confident 'Ich warte' seems to carry infinitely more conviction than the frantic applause with which the assembled Gülleners greet the Mayor's rousing speech.

Zweiter Akt: The complication

Act II of a three-act play is notoriously difficult from a dramatist's point of view. The first act offers ample opportunity to capture the audience's attention, with characters to be introduced, relationships to be explored and so on. Having developed the plot and situation to an interesting, even critical stage by the end of Act I, the playwright must next find ways of maintaining and consolidating his hold on the spectators during the lull which generally precedes the excitement of the concluding act. Common devices to achieve this end include the introduction in Act II of a new character or strand in the plot, or perhaps the development of a sub-plot. Dürrenmatt's bold yet masterly solution to the problem involves no such measures. Instead, having brought his plot to such a violent and very early climax with Claire's offer of vast wealth in exchange for Ill's murder, he now capitalises on the intrinsic drama of the events he has set in train, simply allowing matters to run their course; and the mounting sense of inevitability which propels the play through to its conclusion is indeed an excellent measure of the niceness of his calculations. Meanwhile, Claire's 'Ich warte' constitutes, as it were, a pre-emptive strike against the apparently unavoidable anti-climax in Act II. The finality of her words sets the tone for the next stage in the plot and allows Dürrenmatt, in effect, to make a virtue of a necessity, so that when the curtain rises for the start of the second act, we are already disposed to be expectant yet patient.

Dürrenmatt has cast Claire Zachanassian in the role of interloper, or intruder, a familiar figure in drama whose introduction into a hitherto settled or closed social group, invariably with disruptive effects, is a stock device of tragedy and comedy alike. One need only think of, say, the sitcom arrival of an attractive new neighbour in an apartment block, and the reactions of the previously happily married couple next door, in order to understand the circumstances and the processes involved and to appreciate the scope for serious as well as light-hearted exploitation which they offer the playwright. In Claire, Dürrenmatt has created one of the most compelling and memorable interlopers ever encountered in the theatre, and *Der Besuch der alten Dame* provides a textbook example of how to use such a character to the greatest possible effect.

We would normally expect a character functioning as an interloper to burst into the midst of the target community with violent results, and this is precisely what appears to be happening in Act I of *Der Besuch der alten Dame*. As we saw, Dürrenmatt squeezes every last ounce of impact out of Claire's impending visit, making the audience share the Gülleners' excitement and building up the tension of anticipation in the early part of the first scene, only to take them (Gülleners and audience alike) completely–and explosively–by surprise by her premature arrival. Throughout the first act, however, and despite the setback of being caught unawares at the station, the Gülleners continue to believe that Claire Zachanassian is still Kläri Wäscher at heart. In other words, after their initial shock when she arrives, for the most part they relax and think of her as an exotic oddity rather than as a menacing stranger or intruder. The fact that, as a Güllener born and bred, Claire is also an insider who knows their every weakness, escapes them; and not until the courtroom scene in the Golden Apostle, and even then only to a limited extent, do they begin to perceive her as a threat and go on their guard again.

An interloper can influence the target group by a constant flow of words and deeds, or perhaps, as is the case with Claire, by functioning as a catalyst, starting a chain reaction and then allowing it to run its course. The latter, more subtle approach, calls for a shrewd grasp of group psychology and group dynamics on the part of the dramatist if it is to be convincing, and Dürrenmatt has brought considerable skill and ingenuity to bear in fashioning Claire into the catalyst *par excellence*. To adopt a different metaphor: it is not Husband Number VII who is the expert angler, but Claire, and having dangled the bait in Act I, in Act II she need only await the inevitable nibble; and as we shall see in a moment, Dürrenmatt has also found a most ingenious scenic mode of conveying her waiting role throughout the act.

The focal point throughout the early part of the second act is Ill's shop, a general store in the small-town manner. It is morning, a few days after the banquet-cum-trial in the Golden Apostle. In the background stands the hotel, and the two gangsters, Roby and Toby, can be seen taking mourning wreaths inside. The wreaths provide a clever link between the previous act and the present one:

> ILL: Kränze.
> DER SOHN: Jeden Morgen bringen sie die vom Bahnhof.
> ILL: Für den leeren Sarg im Goldenen Apostel.
> DER SOHN: Schüchtert niemand ein.
> ILL: Das Städtchen steht zu mir. (51)

As well as reminding the audience of Claire's outrageous accoutrements, Ill's words vividly recall the night of her arrival in Güllen and the Mayor's brave speech. Solidarity was then, and is now, the order of the day.

Solidarity also seems to rule within his family, if Ill is to be believed. His wife, 'eine gute Mutter', is unfortunately too tired to come down for breakfast, but his son and daughter, 'gute Kinder, brave

Kinder' (52), simply have no time to hang around, for they must be off: his son hopes to bring in some money by doing casual work at the station, and his daughter is heading for the labour exchange.

As an emotional Ill watches his children depart, we become aware of guitar music and voices from the hotel balcony. Claire, already firmly established as a woman of many parts, can be heard issuing grotesque instructions to her butler: 'Reich mir mein linkes Bein herüber, Boby.... Hinter den Verlobungsblumen auf der Kommode.' A little later on, she will reinforce her bolt-together image and further amuse the audience with, 'Ich bin wieder montiert' (54). She will continue to sit aloft, a lowering presence, for the whole of this act, studiously ignoring the goings-on down below and demonstrating, by a variety of words and deeds, just how powerful, how well connected and how aloof she is from the petty activities of Güllen. Visually, the effect that is gradually produced, helped along by the Teacher's earlier comparison of Claire with Clotho, is of an enormous widow spider who, having spun her web, now waits calmly for her prey to become inextricably ensnared.

Down below, in the shop, Ill goes about his daily business as a series of customers come and go, their conversations alternating with snatches of dialogue from the balcony. The first customer has come for his daily pack of cigarettes: not the usual ones, however, but the dearer ones in the green packet; and he wants them on the slate: 'Schreiben's auf' (53). Ill agrees, mindful of the need to maintain solidarity: 'Weil Sie es sind, Hofbauer, und weil wir zusammenhalten müssen.' Ill's next customers, two housewives, also want their shopping on tick: milk–but 'Vollmilch' (54), and two litres each rather than the usual one; butter; the more expensive white bread instead of black; and chocolate to eat there and then in the shop: 'Bei Ihnen ist es am schönsten, Herr Ill' (55).

A pattern is evolving, discernible to the audience much sooner than to Ill, who so badly needs to believe in the Gülleners' support: 'Sie hat sich verrechnet,' he reassures himself. 'Ich bin ein alter Sünder, Hofbauer, wer ist dies nicht. Es war ein böser Jugendstreich, den ich ihr spielte, doch wie da alle den Antrag abgelehnt haben, die Güllener im Goldenen Apostel, einmütig, trotz dem Elend, war's die schönste Stunde in meinem Leben' (56).

Now that we can see what is happening, Dürrenmatt inflicts another twist of the screw on us, turning the–from the dramatist's point of view–inherently risky sluggishness of the situation to his own advantage by using it to build up tension. When yet another customer comes in demanding credit and better-quality goods (this time imported tobacco and French cognac at almost seven times the price of his customary local schnaps), we ache with apprehension on behalf of the unsuspecting, long-suffering Ill.

At last, however, Ill's own suspicions are aroused by, of all things, the latest customer's feet. He is wearing new yellow shoes, and so, Ill discovers, looking round his shop, are all the other customers. Ill is aghast, for though he is bound to ask how they have been able to afford them, he already knows full well within himself the answer to his question:

> DIE FRAUEN: Wir ließen's aufschreiben, Herr Ill, wir ließen's aufschreiben.
> ILL: Ihr ließet's aufschreiben. Auch bei mir ließet ihr's aufschreiben. Besseren Tabak, bessere Milch, Kognak. Warum habt ihr denn auf einmal Kredit in den Geschäften?
> DER ZWEITE: Bei dir haben wir ja auch Kredit.
> ILL: Womit wollt ihr zahlen?
> *Schweigen. Er beginnt die Kundschaft mit Waren zu bewerfen. Alle flüchten.*
> ILL: Womit wollt ihr zahlen? Womit wollt ihr zahlen? Womit? Womit? (60)

Ill's outburst comes as a welcome release from the pent-up emotion of waiting, not just for the audience, but also for Ill, who has been alone with his thoughts since the night of the banquet. From the replies of the two women shoppers it is evident that they have not even considered the sinister implications of their new style of shopping, but for Ill, the connection is becoming all too clear. His belief in solidarity seems to have been illusory, for the price of Güllen's financial recovery is none other than the price on his head.

On the other hand, with the issue at last out in the open, Ill is in a position to take remedial action, and he turns first, instinctively, to the Policeman. His demand that Claire Zachanassian be arrested, however, meets with an impenetrable mixture of pomposity and twisted logic:

> ILL: Verhaften Sie die Dame auf der Stelle.
> DER POLIZIST: Das heißt, Sie wollen die Dame anzeigen. Ob sie dann verhaftet wird, entscheidet die Polizei. Hat sie was verbrochen?
> ILL: Sie fordert die Einwohner unserer Stadt auf, mich zu töten.
> DER POLIZIST: Und nun soll ich die Dame einfach verhaften. (61f.)

According to the Policeman's tortuous argument, Claire cannot possibly mean her proposition to be taken seriously, because nobody in his right mind pays that much for a murder: 'Nun kann der Vorschlag nicht ernst gemeint sein, weil der Preis von einer Milliarde übertrieben ist, das müssen Sie doch selber zugeben, für so was bietet man tausend oder vielleicht zweitausend, mehr bestimmt nicht,... was wiederum beweist, daß der Vorschlag nicht ernst gemeint war, und sollte er ernst gemeint sein, so kann die Polizei die Dame nicht ernst nehmen, weil sie dann verrückt ist: Kapiert?' (62f.).

In the absence of any real attempt to harm him, the Policeman concludes, he is powerless to act; and in any case, all the signs, from the Gülleners' show of support for Ill in the Golden Apostle to their increased use of his shop, make it plain that no one has any intention of carrying out Claire's demand. 'Freuen Sie sich doch!' he advises Ill. 'Ihr Geschäft geht ja dann besser' (63).

But suddenly the penny drops. The Policeman is wearing new yellow shoes too, just like the others; and drinking better beer as well. He has even acquired 'einen neuen blitzenden Goldzahn' (65). No crime has been committed, 'Kein Mensch bedroht Sie,' the Policeman reminds Ill, but even as he talks he is loading his gun, and his assurance that he is there to protect the public has a hollow ring to it. Ill sums up the situation with uncharacteristic succinctness:

> Die Stadt macht Schulden. Mit den Schulden steigt der Wohlstand. Mit dem Wohlstand die Notwendigkeit, mich zu töten. Und so braucht die Dame nur auf ihrem Balkon zu sitzen, Kaffee zu trinken, Zigarren zu rauchen und zu warten. Nur zu warten.

Pointing his gun at Ill, the Policeman concludes the interview with the announcement that Claire Zachanassian's 'lapdog', the black panther, is loose and must be hunted down. The connection is at once apparent: there are two quarries: the real panther and Ill, Claire's black panther of old. 'Mich jagt ihr, mich,' cries Ill (66).

Ill's next port of call is the town hall. The Mayor has an architect's drawing hanging on the wall, better cigars, a silk tie and new shoes, and a revolver on his desk, but he listens sympathetically enough to Ill reeling off his worries. With Frau Zachanassian's black panther on the loose, he explains, one needs a weapon; indeed, he has summoned all the men of the town who own guns, and as a precaution, the children are being kept in school.

As to Ill's request for protection, the Mayor is extremely disappointed. Theirs is a law-abiding country, and Güllen, he must remind Ill, is a city 'mit humanistischer Tradition' (69): Goethe spent the night here, Brahms composed a quartet. 'Diese Werte,' he adds inconsequentially, 'verpflichten.' He feels deeply hurt by Ill's negative attitude and his lack of trust in the community, and his suggestion that Claire should be arrested he finds quite remarkable; after all, her behaviour is understandable enough, he reminds Ill bluntly: 'Sie haben schließlich zwei Burschen zu Meineid angestiftet und ein Mädchen ins nackte Elend gestoßen' (70). The Gülleners may have condemned Claire's proposition, he continues, but that does not mean that they approve of the crimes which led to her making the proposition. In view of his past immoral deeds, Ill has no right to ask for Claire's arrest; and furthermore, he has forfeited the chance to become mayor: 'Für den Posten eines Bürgermeisters sind gewisse Forderungen sittlicher Natur zu stellen, die Sie nicht mehr erfüllen, das müssen Sie einsehen' (70f.). The less said about the whole sordid affair by all concerned, the better. Ill disagrees: speaking up is his only chance of escaping. But when Ill claims that one–any one of them–is liable to kill him, the Mayor stands on his outraged dignity: 'Gegen diese Verleumdung protestiere ich im Namen der Stadt feierlich.' Obviously, then, when patent truth is dismissed as 'slander', no help will be forthcoming from the civil authorities. 'Ihr habt mich schon zum Tode verurteilt,' Ill cries out in desperation; and to his mind the architect's drawing on the wall is proof enough, for is it not a design for a new town hall?

Ill's last refüge is the vestry. 'Das Gotteshaus steht jedem offen,' the Clergyman assures him (73), but his appearance belies his words of welcome, for he too has a hunting rifle slung over his shoulder. If the Mayor's conversation was informed by the cynicism of a seasoned politician, the Clergyman's is characterised primarily by fatuousness. It appears that when the chips are down, the professional dispenser of spiritual succour can offer only platitudes which evade the practical issues. His advice to his terrified visitor is to worry about his eternal soul instead of his mortal body, to conquer 'the hell within him' and to stop judging others by his own misdeeds:

> Man soll nicht die Menschen fürchten, sondern Gott, nicht den Tod des Leibes, den der Seele.... Weil Sie ein Mädchen um Geld verraten haben, einst vor vielen Jahren, glauben Sie, auch die Menschen würden Sie nun um Geld verraten. Sie schließen von sich selbst auf andere. (74)

To complete his display of impotence, the Clergyman admits to Ill that he can suggest no practical remedies, only prayer and repentance: 'Wir vermögen nichts anderes' (75). Then, ironically, he breaks off his ineffectual counselling of the one member of his flock who is in dire need of support, in order to 'discharge his office' by admitting a new soul to the 'safety' of the Church; and the tolling of bells for the christening service delivers proof positive that he, too, has succumbed to Claire's offer and understands full well the consequences if Ill stays:

> *Die Feuerglocke beginnt zu bimmeln.... Eine zweite Glocke beginnt zu läuten.*
> ILL: Eine zweite Glocke?
> DER PFARRER: Der Ton ist hervorragend. Nicht? Voll und kräftig. Positiv, nur positiv.
> ILL: *schreit auf.* Auch Sie, Pfarrer! Auch Sie!
> DER PFARRER: *wirft sich gegen Ill und umklammert ihn.* Flieh! Wir sind schwach, Christen und Heiden. Flieh, die Glocke dröhnt in Güllen, die Glocke des Verrates. Flieh, führe uns nicht in Versuchung, indem du bleibst. (75f.)

The Clergyman's words are a blend of blasphemy, hypocrisy and unconscious irony: blasphemy in directing a passage from the Lord's Prayer ('Lead us not into temptation') at a mere mortal; hypocrisy in implying that Ill could somehow be responsible for their lack of moral fibre; and irony, no doubt unintentional, in the words, 'die Glocke dröhnt', a familiar phrase which of course calls to mind the title of Ernest Hemingway's novel, but also, and more inportantly, the original source, a valedictory poem by John Donne entitled *Devotions*: 'Any man's death diminishes me, because I am involved in mankind; And therefore never send to know for whom the bell tolls; it tolls for thee.' The same poem also contains another oft-quoted phrase, 'No man is an island, entire of itself,' and the implications of the reference are plain: a death is looming in Güllen, but with it also a day of reckoning of both a personal and a collective nature, in spite of the Clergyman's feeble attempts to saddle Ill with the responsibility for the impending actions of himself and the other members of his community; feeble, because advice from a Clergyman which is directed towards saving *his* soul, rather than that of the member of his flock who seeks the advice, must surely be considered at best feeble, at worst despicable.

At this point, two shots ring out: Claire's black panther has been killed. Thinking the shots are intended for him, Ill collapses on the ground, whilst the Clergyman cowers down beside him, urging him again to flee. When he finally gets to his feet and departs, he takes the Clergyman's gun with him.

As we remarked earlier, Claire spends the whole of Act II sitting on her hotel balcony, able to observe the goings-on down below, but taking no part in them. At regular intervals, the action switches to the balcony, where Claire is engaged in a variety of activities of a sort quite alien to the experience of the Gülleners, ranging from reminiscing about her former husbands ('Mein vierter.... Verführte ihn im Buckingham Palast' (66)) through discussing the glittering guest list for her eighth wedding ('Onassis kommt. Der Herzog und die

Herzogin. Aga.... Der ganze Rivierakram' (72)) to conducting top-level financial transactions and political negotiations, such as dismissing the President of the World Bank, who has just flown in from New York to consult her ('Ich bin nicht zu sprechen. Er soll wieder zurückfliegen' (68)). Everything she says and does is calculated to impress upon us the immense power she wields world-wide, and her supreme indifference to the trivial events unfolding at ground level–whether by her mock-lyrical description of the idyllic view (55), repeated parrot-fashion a little later on by Husband Number VIII (58); her blasé treatment of marriage and divorce (*passim*); her constant name-dropping and nonchalant tycoonery (61, 62 *et passim*); or, when Ill turns on his customers and accuses them of incurring debts at the expense of his life, the studied casualness of her callous *double-entendre*: 'Man wird sich um den Fleischpreis streiten' (60). Yet we know full well, of course, that her indifference is anything but genuine. She may not be participating in the conflict over Ill, but she is certainly an acutely interested observer.

The death of her panther now brings the hitherto separate worlds of Claire and the Gülleners together for a few brief moments. On hearing the shots, she asks what is going on; and when told that her pet is lying dead (significantly) outside Ill's shop, her only comment is characteristically hard-bitten: 'Schade um das Tierchen' (76); but the Gülleners gather outside the hotel and the Teacher, eager to please as always, musters his choir once more to sing a dirge, preceded by a typically long-winded oration: 'Wir sind aus einer großen Gefahr errettet worden. Der schwarze Panther schlich unheilbrütend durch unsere Gassen. Doch wenn wir auch befreit aufatmen, so beklagen wir dennoch den Tod einer so kostbaren zoologischen Rarität....' (77).

Just as the choir is starting to sing, however, Ill bursts on the scene, armed with the Clergyman's gun, and announces that the dirge is intended not for the panther, but for him. He sends the Gülleners packing, Claire tells Husband Number VIII to make himself scarce, and she and Ill are alone together. If the Teacher's choir, assembled beneath Claire's balcony, at first gave the incongruous impression that they were about to sing a serenade, the scene before us now recalls, no less incongruously, *Romeo and Juliet*. Indeed, Claire fosters this image by reminding Ill tenderly of the not entirely dissimilar circumstances of their first meeting: 'Ich war auch auf einem Balkon, damals.... Und du standst da und du schautest hinauf zu mir, immerzu....' (78).

Claire came down from the balcony then, she remembers, and silently, hand in hand, they went to the edge of town, and–once Ill had chased away his hangers-on, Koby and Loby–'wir waren allein'

(79). But their love affair is history, and in the here and now she and Ill are just talking past one another, as he desperately begs her to tell him that what is happening is all just a cruel joke and, pointing his gun at her, declares he will stop at nothing to save his own skin. Neither heeds what the other is saying, for what we are witnessing is two monologues, not a dialogue at all, and their brief exchange ends with Ill impotently lowering his gun and Claire awakening from her reverie and calling for her butler to take her indoors.

The scene shifts to the station platform once more. Significantly, there are already unmistakable signs of economic upturn, such as a new timetable and a holiday poster on the wall, and evidence of building work going on in the distance. Ill arrives with a suitcase, and as if from nowhere, Gülleners appear all around him: he is leaving and they have come to see him off. Yet to Ill's over-wrought mind their very presence is menacing, and he derives no comfort from their bland assurances that they mean him no harm. When they discover that he is planning to emigrate to Australia, they mock him and remind him of the dangers of such a move: one of the little eunuchs did exactly that, after all. He will be much safer staying in Güllen.

When Ill's train arrives, a curious thing happens: his fellow-citizens crowd round him, wishing him a safe journey and the like, but he does not get on board. No one moves, no one lays a finger on him, yet he cannot bring himself to pass through the crowd to the waiting train. They urge him to go, but he is rooted to the spot, scared stiff, and eventually his knees give away. 'Einer wird mich zurückhalten, wenn ich den Zug besteige,' he is convinced (84), and though everyone denies it, he remains motionless and the train sets off without him. The Gülleners wander off, their mission accomplished, leaving Ill alone, in a state of collapse, to utter the final words of the act: 'Ich bin verloren' (85). It is significant that his collapse should occur at the railway station, the point of arrival in and departure from Güllen: the train is Güllen's link with the outside world, but the only character free to come and go at will is Claire.

The question obviously arises: why does Ill stay? Dürrenmatt leaves the matter nicely ambiguous. Certainly Ill is terrified that his fellow-citizens will forcibly restrain him from boarding the train, despite their protestations of goodwill, and it may be that he opts for the slightly more remote threat to his person implicit in his remaining in Güllen, in preference to what he perceives as certain death should he attempt to depart. (The most remote threat of all, that he will be pursued and punished in Australia, is completely overshadowed in his mind by the immediate danger of running the gauntlet of his fellow

Gülleners). On the other hand, although the Gülleners undoubtedly want Ill to stay in Güllen, there is no evidence that they would have actually harmed him or even restrained him physically if he had headed for the waiting train.

Dürrenmatt, in fact, leaves us in no doubt that at this stage in the play the Gülleners have no evil designs on Ill, though they are of course already on the slippery slope of easy credit. Commenting on this scene in *Anmerkung I*, he writes: 'Sie sind nicht böse zu zeichnen, durchaus nicht; zuerst entschlossen, das Angebot abzulehnen, machen sie nun Schulden, doch nicht im Vorsatz, Ill zu töten, sondern aus Leichtsinn, aus einem Gefühl heraus, es lasse sich alles schon arrangieren. So ist der zweite Akt zu inszenieren. Auch die Bahnhofszene. Die Furcht ist bei Ill allein, der seine Lage begreift, noch fällt kein böses Wort, erst die Szene in der Peterschen Scheune [the first scene of Act III] bringt die Wendung. Das Verhängnis ist nicht mehr zu umgehen' (143).

But if the Gülleners do not yet realise what is going to happen, Ill certainly does, and indeed has done so for some considerable time; and if, as Dürrenmatt suggests, for the Gülleners the turning-point has yet to come, for Ill it is already long past. Although the text contains nothing specific to support the theory, it is tempting to speculate that in this final scene of Act II, Ill is already subconsciously squaring up to what will eventually emerge as the central issue of the play: the question of personal responsibility. As we shall see in due course, Dürrenmatt neatly apportions responsibility between Ill on the one hand and his fellow-citizens on the other: Ill is responsible for the injustice which was done to Claire, but the people of Güllen must be held responsible for the death of Ill. Arguably, Ill's failure to board the train is due as much to a subconscious acknowledgement that it is his moral duty to stay and face the music, as to the fear of being attacked. And perhaps, too, he is prompted to stay by an inner resolve to make the Gülleners pay for the debts they have so casually incurred, a refusal to let them off the moral hook by conveniently running away. Erwin Jaeckle summed up the situation perfectly in a short note for the 1977 performance of *Der Besuch der alten Dame* in Zürich: '[Es geht um Ill,] der sich inmitten von Versagen und Schuld zu achten beginnt, den einfachen Mann, "dem langsam etwas aufgeht", ... den bisher Gedankenlosen, der die Gerechtigkeit an sich erlebt.... Er zwingt die Güllener zur Folgerightigkeit. Er tut es als Einzelner, also nicht mehr als Güllener.'[3]

3 *Programmheft* des Schauspielhauses Zürich, June 1977, 29.

Dritter Akt The final climax and dénouement

The scene which greets the audience, when the play resumes after the interval, is a bizarre one: Claire Zachanassian, wearing a white wedding dress, is sitting motionless in her sedan-chair in the middle of the *Petersche Scheune*. She is surrounded by farmyard lumber–old carts, bales of straw, etc.–and from the rafters hang, appropriately, huge spiders' webs. To an English audience, her appearance might recall Miss Havisham, the jilted bride in Dickens' *Great Expectations*, who spent the rest of her life in her wedding dress, brooding over her wedding cake.

Claire, however, far from being a jilted bride, has just retired to the barn for a rest after her latest wedding in the cathedral. Now she receives a deputation: the Doctor and the Teacher. As Güllen's two lay intellectuals, they hope to use their powers of persuasion to change Claire's mind. They laboriously explain the obvious, that the people of Güllen are in a dilemma: on the one hand they have incurred massive debts which must be paid for, but on the other they have their 'abendländischen Prinzipien' (88), which forbid them to take Ill's life. The Teacher outlines their rescue plan: if, for a much more modest investment than the billion she has offered, Claire will help put Güllen on its feet again by buying up the town's defunct factories and getting them back in production, the townspeople will be able to clear their debts. Being decent, reasonable people, they do not doubt that Claire will see the merits of their argument and acquiesce.

Claire even leads them on for a moment by agreeing that their proposal makes good business sense, only to dash their hopes by announcing that it is impossible to carry it out: 'Ich kann die Platz-an-der-Sonne-Hütte nicht kaufen, weil sie mir schon gehört' (89). She owns the other factories too; to be precise, Claire owns Güllen lock, stock and barrel, and as a vital element in her master plan, she has been systematically sabotaging the town's economy: 'Ließ den Plunder aufkaufen durch meine Agenten, die Betriebe stillegen' (90). Her motives are plain and unambiguous, her authority total, her determination unswerving: she is intent on revenge. When she was forced to leave Güllen, young, defenceless and pregnant, she vowed to return one day: 'Nun bin ich da. Nun stelle ich die Bedingungen, diktiere das Geschäft.'

The Doctor, rendered almost speechless, can only gasp at the monstrousness of Claire's bombshell revelation. The Teacher, never lost for words, makes one last appeal to her better nature: 'Lassen Sie den unheilvollen Gedanken der Rache fallen, treiben Sie uns nicht zum Äußersten,' he implores her. 'Helfen Sie armen, schwachen, aber rechtschaffenen Leuten, ein etwas würdigeres Leben zu führen, ringen Sie sich zur reinen Menschlichkeit durch!' (90f.) But this is mere empty rhetoric, and Claire's parting shot, as she is borne off back to town in her sedan-chair, confirm that she is every inch the realist:

> Die Menschlichkeit, meine Herren, ist für die Börse der Millionäre geschaffen, mit meiner Finanzkraft leistet man sich eine Weltordnung. Die Welt machte mich zur Hure, nun mache ich sie zu einem Bordell. Anständig ist nur, wer zahlt, und ich zahle. Güllen für einen Mord, Konkjunktur für eine Leiche.

This marks the turning-point for the Gülleners to which Dürrenmatt refers in *Anmerkung I*. Humanity stands revealed as a luxury which the Gülleners simply cannot afford. Having chosen prosperity, they must now pay for it. They have no option but to murder Ill, yet to enable them to live with themselves, they must find ways of salving their consciences. The process involves identifying, ostracising and finally eradicating a victim who can be made to shoulder whatever blame might otherwise attach to them. The first stage has already occurred: Ill has been a marked man ever since the night of the banquet. The second stage, in which the townspeople draw closer together to form a community from which Ill is specifically excluded, begins now, with the Doctor's horrified question, 'Mein Gott, was sollen wir tun?', and the Teacher's reply: 'Was uns das Gewissen vorschreibt, Doktor Nüßlin.' In the remainder of the play, we are about to witness the elimination of a scapegoat.

For the Gülleners, obeying their consciences means in practice associating themselves with Claire's indictment of Ill, distancing themselves increasingly from him and viewing him with ever-mounting righteous indignation: 'Von nun an bereiten sich die Güllener allmählich auf die Ermordung vor, entrüsten sich über Ills Schuld usw.' (Dürrenmatt, *Anmerkung I*, 143f.). Frau Ill is the first to experience the Gülleners' new *esprit de corps*, in the scene which follows Claire's meeting with the Teacher and the Doctor in the *Petersche Scheune*:

> DER ERSTE: Ihr Mann, Frau Ill? Sah ihn lange nicht.... Das schlechte Gewissen. Schlimm hat er's mit der armen Frau Zachanassian getrieben....
> DER ZWEITE: Ein Mädchen ins Unglück stürzen. Pfui Teufel. (93)

This exchange takes place in Ill's shop. There is mounting evidence of prosperity, in the customers' clothes and their purchases, but also in the appearance of the shop itself: there is a new sign outside, a gleaming new counter, a new till, etc. Ironically, even the prospective victim is benefitting from the town's new-found wealth. Significantly, though, the Gülleners are still buying on tick: for they can now afford to do so with an easy mind, since they know within themselves that Ill is going to be killed; and also with a clear conscience, thanks to their growing conviction that bailing Güllen out with his life is no more than Ill deserves.

In Act I, when Claire Zachanassian arrived in Güllen, she left her following of *paparazzi* lunching obliviously on the train: 'Laß sie weiterdinieren,' she said at that time. 'Ich brauche die Presse fürs erste nicht in Güllen. Und später wird sie schon kommen' (24). Now the media are beginning to assemble in Güllen, and with their arrival Dürrenmatt introduces a new motif: the uneasy relationship between news-gathering and truth. The reporters have no inkling of what is really going on in Güllen, nor will they ever know; following Claire's activities is just a routine assignment which they must make as newsworthy as possible by finding, or if necessary inventing, interesting 'angles'. With practised ease they fabricate an entire love story around Claire, Ill and his wife:

> PRESSEMANN I: Wir können uns die Romanze vorstellen: Herr Ill und Claire Zachanassian wachsen zusammen auf, sind vielleicht Nachbarskinder, gehen gemeinsam in die Schule, Spaziergänge in den Wald, die ersten Küsse und so weiter, bis Herr Ill Sie kennenlernt, gute Frau, als das Neue, das Ungewohnte, als die Leidenschaft.
> FRAU ILL: Es ist genau so passiert, wie Sie es erzählen.
> PRESSEMANN I: Claire Zachanassian begreift, verzichtet auf ihre stille, edle Art, und Sie heiraten–
> FRAU ILL: Aus Liebe....
> PRESSEMANN I: Aus Liebe. (96f.)

When they come to take Ill's photograph, Dürrenmatt employs heavy dramatic irony and the reporter displays his profound ignorance of the situation in Güllen by asking Ill to pretend to sell the Butcher an axe, so as to enliven his picture:

> Lebensmittel, Haushaltgegenstände, Eisenwaren–Am besten: Verkaufen Sie das Beil.... Dem Metzger. *Demonstriert.* Sie nehmen das Beil, wiegen es in der Hand, machen ein nachdenkliches Gesicht, sehen Sie, so; und Sie, Herr Ill, neigen sich über den Ladentisch, reden dem Metzger zu. Bitte. *Er arrangiert die Stellung.* Natürlicher, meine Herren, ungezwungener. (100)

But irrespective of the journalists' total lack of regard for the truth, the townspeople do of course share a guilty secret, and are therefore hostile towards the press. Their prime concern is that someone will talk. They think they can rely on the Clergyman, but Ill, 'bei seinem Charakter' (93), is a different matter, and if he tries to pretend that Claire has put a price on his head, they mutter, they will be forced to take action: not because of her promised money, of course, but 'aus Volkszorn'. The use of emotive expressions such as this, and the implication that Ill is a thoroughly bad lot, play an important part in fostering that sense of corporate identity by means of which the target individual is systematically and remorselessly isolated from his former friends and fellows.

For a time, the Butcher stands guard at the foot of the stairs, as if to prevent Ill from meeting the reporters, but the Gülleners have in fact less to fear from his loose tongue than from that of one of their own number, the Teacher. When the latter enters the shop, he is as pompous as ever–'Ich benötige ein starkes alkoholisches Getränk'–, but visibly shaken. After downing several glasses of schnaps in quick succession, he gains Dutch courage and proclaims that it is time for the gentlemen of the press to know the truth: 'Ungeheuerliche Dinge bereiten sich vor in Güllen!' (99). His speech is stopped short by an assured and unexpected 'Schweigen Sie' from Ill, who has just come downstairs. Apologising to the reporters, Ill explains that the Teacher is drunk. Their attention shifts to taking Ill's photograph, and immediately afterwards, to underline the fact that the Gülleners need not have worried unduly about the Teacher's outburst being heeded by the journalists, they go charging off to follow up the latest titbit of news, that Claire has produced yet another husband.

Left alone with Ill, the Gülleners can speak more freely, and we witness a thuggish element beginning to creep into the behaviour of these hitherto decent, seemingly innocuous men:

> *Der Zweite ... bleibt ... noch vor Ill stehen, bevor er hinausgeht.*
> DER ZWEITE: Klug, äußerst klug, keinen Unsinn zu schwatzen.
> DER DRITTE: Einem Halunken wie dir würde man ja auch kein Wort glauben. *Er geht.*
> *Der Vierte spuckt aus, geht ebenfalls....*
> DER ERSTE: Offen gesagt: Was Sie Klärchen angetan haben, tut nur ein Schuft. (101)

Ill and the Teacher are now alone together. What follows is the moment of truth, for Güllen, as represented by the Teacher, and also for Ill. Acknowledging the evil hold which Claire has on them all, the Teacher tries to persuade Ill to enlist the aid of the press and fight for his life. Ill, however, has already decided otherwise. He does not propose to fight any longer, because he no longer considers he has any rights: 'Ich bin schließlich schuld daran.... Ich habe Klara zu dem gemacht, was sie ist, und mich zu dem, was ich bin, ein verschmierter windiger Krämer. Was soll ich tun, Lehrer von Güllen? Den Unschuldigen spielen? Alles ist meine Tat.... Ich kann mir nicht mehr helfen und auch euch nicht mehr' (102f.).

The Teacher's reply is as usual verbose, but nevertheless correct. He agrees that Ill is right: 'Sie haben recht.... Sie sind schuld an allem. Man wird Sie töten.... Auch ich werde mitmachen' (103). But, fleshing out the implications of Ill's 'auch euch nicht mehr', he predicts repercussions for the people of Güllen long after the contract with Claire is completed: as they will then be no less culpable than Ill, they too must one day face judgement and retribution for the crime they are about to commit: 'Noch weiß ich, daß auch zu uns einmal eine alte Dame kommen wird, eines Tages, und daß dann mit uns geschehen wird, was nun mit Ihnen geschieht.' His confession completed, he asks Ill for another bottle of schnaps and, as proof that he too has capitulated to Claire's demands, leaves the shop with the words, Schreiben Sie sie auf.'[4]

The Ill of Act III is in many respects a new man, even though also a condemned man. He is altogether more self-assured than before, and seems to have gained in stature. He is preparing himself, spiritually and emotionally, for his coming ordeal, and as part of this process he needs to make his peace with his family and with Claire, and to take his leave of them. Wistfully, but a little reproachfully too, he takes stock of the signs of prosperity all around him–a shop the likes of which he has only ever dreamed of; a daughter who takes tennis lessons instead of going to the labour exchange; a wife with a new fur coat in her wardrobe; and a son with a car–and he cannot escape the fact that they, too, have betrayed him for money. Nevertheless, they are his kith and kin, and so he announces his wish: to enjoy a share of the family's good fortune, just once, by going for a drive in the country in the new car.

Whilst the others are putting on their best clothes for the outing, Ill receives a final visit from the Mayor. He has brought a loaded pistol, hoping that even at this stage Ill will spare the townspeople the dirty work by shooting himself. Ill, with his new-found confidence, politely declines: 'Ich brauche es nicht' (106). Rather awkwardly, but with great courtesy, the Mayor next proceeds to discuss the arrangements

4 For his studio version of *Der Besuch der alten Dame* in Bern in December, 1959, Dürrenmatt drastically shortened the Teacher's final speech and made explicit the sea-change that comes over him: before his final 'Schreiben Sie sie auf', he says: 'Und nun will ich Ihnen etwas sagen, Alfred Ill, etwas Grundsätzliches.... Sie sind ein Schuft, Ill, nichts weiter' (152). This is extremely well-judged by Dürrenmatt. Not only is it appropriate that at this, his moment of truth, the Teacher should drop his usual verbose way of talking for once, and say 'something basic', but what he says is so basic, so vulgar and therefore so shockingly at odds with the image he has always cultivated, that it reveals that, for all his preaching about humanist values etc., there lurks within him as thuggish a streak as there is in any of the others.

for the assembly of the townspeople which is scheduled for that evening. The Gülleners are to meet in the solemn setting of the *Theatersaal* in the Golden Apostle Hotel to 'deal with Ill's case', as he euphemistically puts it. The Mayor's difficulty in planning the evening is that he does not know how Ill will behave in the event, which he tries to assure Ill is remote, that the Gülleners decide to accept Claire's proposition. Cautiously, he puts the crucial question: 'In diesem Fall, würden Sie den Urteilsspruch annehmen, Ill? Die Presse ist nämlich dabei.'

The Mayor's mention of the press comes as a surprise to Ill. Claire Zachanassian's activities attract publicity, the Mayor explains, and her homecoming and wedding in the cathedral are particularly newsworthy events. Güllen is currently the focus of attention and all the media will be present to report on 'unsere alten demokratischen Einrichtungen', as he wryly describes the forthcoming activities. Ill cannot believe that Claire's proposal is to be made public; nor will it be, the Mayor replies, choosing his words carefully:

> Nicht direkt–nur die Eingeweihten werden den Sinn der Verhandlung verstehen.
> ILL: Daß es um mein Leben geht. (107)

The press will simply be informed that by arrangement with Ill, who as everyone knows was her 'Jugendfreund', Claire wishes to establish a benevolent fund for the Gülleners. Thus Ill will appear blameless, 'whatever happens'; the Mayor is arranging things in this way, he continues, turning nasty, 'nicht Ihnen, sondern Ihrer kreuzbraven, ehrlichen Familie zuliebe, offen gestanden.' Ill has remained silent so far, the Mayor reminds him; but will he continue to be silent? If not, he adds menacingly, they will be forced to deal with everything without a public assembly.

Ill is almost relieved to be threatened openly at last, after so much innuendo–not that the Mayor will admit to threatening Ill. 'Ich drohe Ihnen nicht, Ill, Sie drohen uns,' he retorts, displaying his politician's knack of twisting the facts to his own advantage. But the Mayor need not worry, for Ill's mind is already made up:

> ILL: Ich schweige.
> DER BÜRGERMEISTER: Wie der Beschluß der Versammlung auch ausfällt?
> ILL: Ich nehme ihn an.
> DER BÜRGERMEISTER: Schön. (107f.)

The Mayor, however, cannot resist making one final appeal to Ill's 'honour'. If only he will do the decent thing and shoot himself, the Gülleners will be spared the public ceremony and the execution to follow, and they will still be able to collect the money. But Ill will have none of this. He has been through hell, he tells the Mayor, and entirely by his own efforts he has conquered his fear. Now the Gülleners must be his judges and his executioners. He will not resist, because this, for him, will be justice. Whether it is also justice for Güllen, he adds, is another matter, and does not concern him. The townspeople must make their own decisions and be responsible for their own actions: 'euer Handeln kann ich euch nicht abnehmen' (109). The Mayor's snide parting shot is both unworthy and unconvincing: 'Sie verpassen die Chance, sich reinzuwaschen, ein halbwegs anständiger Mensch zu werden. Doch das kann man von Ihnen ja nicht verlangen.' Our sympathies are by now firmly with Ill, patently the only decent man in Güllen.

Ill's family now join him and they all go for a surreal drive in his son's 'car', represented on stage by four chairs. The scene is laden with pathos, but also not lacking in humour. Ill has longed all his life to own a car like this, and now he wants to savour the feeling just once, and to take one last look at his home town and the country round about. Everywhere he looks, there is evidence of Güllen's economic upturn: houses are being renovated or extended, near-derelict pubs are being turned into restaurants, and the Doctor has bought a new Mercedes. Ill's family, too, have gone up in the world. His son drives with verve and panache, his daughter is taking English and French lessons and studying literature; and she has acquired airs and graces, as her conversation humorously reveals: she passes remarks in French and English, describes the country scene as 'eine Stimmung wie bei Adalbert Stifter' (113) and sneeringly calls someone who overtakes them in a bigger car a *nouveau-riche*.

When the car reaches the *Konradsweilerwald*, Ill gets out and dismisses his family. He wants to spend a little time alone in the forest before walking back to Güllen, where the bells (four of them now) are already tolling to summon the townspeople to the Golden Apostle. The family, curiously–or conveniently–blind to what is going on in their town, bid him a casual 'So long' and drive off to see a film in Kalberstadt. They will not attend the meeting, for Dürrenmatt expressly excludes them from involvement in what happens to Ill: 'Nur die Familie redet sich bis zum Schlusse ein, es komme alles noch gut, auch sie ist nicht böse, nur schwach wie alle' (*Anmerkung I*, 144).

Claire now appears, accompanied by Husband Number IX, the Nobel Prizewinner. She introduces him to Ill, they chat in a desultory way and after a few moments she sends her husband off to look for ruins. The final scene between the ex-lovers can commence. They sit together and smoke, appropriately, Romeo et Juliettes, whilst one of the gangsters plays Ill's favourite tune on the guitar. Eventually Ill breaks the silence, haltingly, to broach at last a subject that has lain dormant for all of forty-five years:

> ILL: Du hattest–ich meine, wir hatten ein Kind?
> CLAIRE ZACHANASSIAN: Gewiß.
> ILL: War es ein Bub oder ein Mädchen?
> CLAIRE ZACHANASSIAN: Ein Mädchen.
> ILL: Und was hast du ihm für einen Namen gegeben?
> CLAIRE ZACHANASSIAN: Geneviève.
> ILL: Hübscher Name.
> CLAIRE ZACHANASSIAN: Ich sah das Ding nur einmal. Bei der Geburt. Dann wurde es genommen. Von der christlichen Fürsorge. (115f.)

The audience senses that here, in this uneasy, poignant conversation about *their* baby, talking about what was and thinking about what might have been, Claire and Ill have finally found reconciliation with one another. It is a perverted sort of reconciliation, to be sure, the product of a warped mind, and the endgame which Claire now outlines is grotesque in the extreme, yet for one fleeting moment we also catch a glimpse of the rightness of it as seen through their eyes:

> ILL: Nun ist es soweit.... Heute abend versammelt sich die Gemeinde. Man wird mich zum Tode verurteilen, und einer wird mich töten. Ich weiß nicht, wer es sein wird und wo es geschehen wird, ich weiß nur, daß ich ein sinnloses Leben beende.
> CLAIRE ZACHANASSIAN: Ich liebte dich. Du hast mich verraten. Doch den Traum von Leben, von Liebe, von Vertrauen, diesen einst wirklichen Traum habe ich nicht vergessen. Ich will ihn wieder errichten mit meinen Milliarden, die Vergangenheit ändern, indem ich dich vernichte.... Ich werde dich in deinem Sarg nach Capri bringen. Ließ ein Mausoleum errichten im Park meines Palazzos. Von Zypressen umgeben. Mit Blick aufs Mittelmeer.
> ILL: Kenne ich nur von Abbildungen.
> CLAIRE ZACHANASSIAN: Tiefblau. Ein grandioses Panorama. Dort wirst du bleiben. Bei mir. (117f.)

With that, Husband Number IX returns, the spell is broken, the meeting is at an end and Claire is carried off in her sedan-chair. The scene we have just witnessed is extremely disquieting, not merely because of the bitter-sweet encounter between two former lovers, but also because, even though we know rationally that no one can turn the clock back, we sense that Claire has just demonstrated her uncanny ability to do precisely that.

For the climactic final scene, Dürrenmatt gives us an entirely new setting: the *Theatersaal* of the Golden Apostle. First, a radio commentator explains to his listeners that the world's press, photographers and film crews have congregated in Güllen for this momentous occasion: having visited Claire's birthplace and interviewed the Clergyman, they are now assembled, in the very hotel where Goethe once spent the night, for a 'civic event'. Frau Zachanassian will not be there in person, but the Mayor will be making an important announcement on her behalf. In keeping with an old custom, the menfolk of Güllen are gathered together on the stage along with the Mayor; the women sit in the auditorium.

The Mayor comes straight to the point: 'Ich habe die Ehre, bekanntgeben zu dürfen, daß Frau Claire Zachanassian, die Tochter unseres bedeutenden Mitbürgers, des Architekten Gottfried Wäscher, beabsichtigt, uns eine Milliarde zu schenken.... Fünfhundert Millionen der Stadt, fünfhundert Millionen an alle Bürger verteilt' (120). Sensational news. This means, the radio announcer informs his listeners, in the superfluous way of radio announcers the world over, that the inhabitants of Güllen are about to become rich overnight. It will be 'eines der größten sozialen Experimente unserer Epoche.'

Now the Teacher addresses the assembly. Like Claire's builder-turned-architect father a moment ago, he has been elevated to 'Rektor des Gymnasiums' (122). In a lengthy oration, replete with lofty phrases, he reminds his fellow-citizens in suitably veiled terms of Claire's motives, and urges them to examine their own before accepting her offer:

> Sie will für ihre Milliarde Gerechtigkeit, die Gerechtigkeit.... Wir duldeten die Ungerechtigkeit.... Es geht nicht um Geld,... es geht darum, ob wir Gerechtigkeit verwirklichen wollen, und nicht nur sie, sondern auch all die Ideale,... die den Wert unseres Abendlandes ausmachen! ... Habt ihr diesen Hunger, Güllener, diesen Hunger des Geistes, und nicht nur den anderen, profanen, den Hunger des Liebes? ... Nur wenn ihr das Böse nicht aushaltet,... dürft ihr die Milliarde der Frau Zachanassian annehmen und die Bedingung erfüllen, die mit dieser Stiftung verbunden ist. (121f.)

The Teacher's rousing speech is punctuated by mounting bursts of applause from the townspeople and the now-familiar platitudes from the announcer: 'Die Rede des Rektors bewies eine sittliche Größe, wie wir sie heute–leider–nicht mehr allzuoft finden' (122). The Mayor next addresses Ill, in the hackneyed words of the broadcaster 'ein rüstiger Mann von etwa siebzig Jahren, ein senkrechter Güllener von altem Schrot und Korn' (123).

Thus far, Ill has continued to sit motionless on the bench where he and Claire met in the forest, while the scenery changed around him. He has been on stage continuously since halfway through the scene in the shop, and his dishevelled appearance and ragged old clothes are now in striking contrast to those of the Gülleners, who are in full evening dress. The Policeman, wearing a resplendent new uniform, has been sitting warder-like next to Ill, and now he gives his charge a shove. The Mayor puts a question to Ill, whom the commentator uncomprehendingly describes as the man at whose suggestion the 'Zachanassian Fund' was set up. The question, like the rest of the proceedings, is cryptic: 'Werden Sie unseren Entscheid über Annahme oder Ablehnung der Claire-Zachanassian-Stiftung respektieren?' When Ill answers in the affirmative, the Mayor moves on to the next phase in the ritual: he gives each of the assembled dignitaries in turn, the Clergyman, the Doctor, the Policeman and the leader of the opposition party, an opportunity to speak. No one says a word.

The preliminaries completed, the Mayor is ready to call for a 'vote': 'Wer reinen Herzens die Gerechtigkeit verwirklichen will, erhebe die Hand' (124). Everyone except Ill raises their hand. Next the citizens swear an oath, repeating the Mayor's words phrase by phrase. Making the naive radio commentator inadvertently hit the nail on the head by describing this part of the proceedings as 'eine gewaltige Verschwörung für eine bessere, gerechtere Welt'–a *conspiracy* to create a better world–is a characteristically sardonic touch on Dürrenmatt's part. The wording of the oath itself, which may perhaps be intended as a parody on the legendary Swiss oath of independence, the *Rütlischwur*, is as follows:

> Die Stiftung der Claire Zachanassian ist angenommen. Einstimmig. Nicht des Geldes–sondern der Gerechtigkeit wegen–und aus Gewissensnot. Denn wir können nicht leben, wenn wir ein Verbrechen unter uns dulden–welches wir ausrotten müssen–damit unsere Seelen nicht Schaden erleiden–und unsere heiligsten Güter. (124f.)

The hypocrisy of the final words is more than Ill can bear, and he cries out in anguish, 'Mein Gott!' At this moment, however, there has been a technical hitch in the filming of the ceremony, and the Gülleners obligingly repeat the entire oath. Only Ill remains silent, thus underlining the contrast between the sincerity of his 'Freudenschrei' (as the cameraman mistakenly interprets it) and the shallowness of the townspeople's responses.

The public ceremony over, the Mayor's next task is to clear the premises of outsiders. He announces that refreshments are being served in the restaurant for the reporters, and tea in the garden for the ladies. With only the men of Güllen left on the stage, the secret part of the proceedings can commence. The doors of the auditorium are locked and the lights are extinguished. By the dim light of the full moon, the men form a double line, at the end of which, looking for all the world like an executioner, stands the Gymnast. Ill, who somehow has not expected the 'sentence' to be carried out straight away, is in a daze. Whilst he smokes his last cigarette, the Clergyman prepares to comfort him: 'Nun, Ill, Ihre schwere Stunde ist gekommen,' he intones sanctimoniously (128). Ill cuts short his attempt at a sermon, and replies curtly to his question, 'Sie fürchten sich nicht?' with 'Nicht mehr sehr.' But at the Clergyman's lame promise that he will pray for Ill, the condemned man's telling injunction, 'Beten Sie für Güllen,' strikes home, and the Clergyman can only join the others, muttering helplessly as he goes: 'Gott sei uns gnädig.'

The Mayor now asks Ill to stand up. The Policeman, not for the first time, loses control of himself and has to be admonished by the Mayor: grunting 'Steh auf, du Schwein,' he drags Ill to his feet (129). After some hesitation, Ill advances slowly into the double line of men, and as their ranks close behind him, goes down on his knees. What happens next is not entirely clear, even from the stage-directions:

> *Ganz hinten stellt sich ihm der Turner entgegen.... Die Gasse [der schweigenden Männer] verwandelt sich in einen Menschenknäuel, lautlos, der sich ballt, der langsam niederkauert. Stille. Von links kommen Journalisten. Es wird hell.... Der Menschenknäuel lockert sich auf. Die Männer sammeln sich im Hintergrund, schweigend. Zurück bleibt nur der Arzt, vor einem Leichnam kniend, über den ein kariertes Tischtuch, wie es in Wirtschaften üblich ist, gebreitet ist. Der Arzt steht auf. Nimmt das Stethoskop ab.* (130)

As instructed by Claire at their first meeting (30), the Doctor dutifully diagnoses heart failure; the Mayor, cynical to the bitter end, adds, 'Tod aus Freude'; and the Reporter, fooled to the end, enthuses: 'Das Leben schreibt die schönsten Geschichten.' But what, then, was the role of the Gymnast, whom Claire asked on the night of the banquet (41) if he had ever strangled anyone? Or was Ill smothered or punched to death by all the men of Güllen? We simply cannot know the answer, but in any case, it does not matter: for the Gülleners, having acted as a group to ostracise Ill, must now bear collective responsibility for his death.

With Ill disposed of, the final moments of the action come as an anti-climax. Claire Zachanassian comes on stage and inspects the body, which is then carried off on a stretcher. Evidently, she has turned the clock back after all by procuring Ill's death: 'Er ist wieder so, wie er war, vor langer Zeit, der schwarze Panther' (131). She hands the mayor a cheque in completion of her part of the contract, and departs for Capri with her bounty.

Schlußbild: The epilogue

Before the final curtain falls on Güllen, Dürrenmatt shows us, in a final tableau, how its citizens have prospered. The stage-directions describe how the standard of living in the town has risen gradually but inexorably in the course of the play, and has now reached its 'apotheosis': '*Die einst graue Welt hat sich in etwas technisch Blitzblankes, in Reichtum verwandelt, mündet in ein Welt-Happy-End ein*' (131f.). We are at the station once more, but it has been renovated, equipped with neon lights and decorated with banners and posters. Dressed as they were on the night of Ill's death, the men of Güllen in tails, the women in evening dresses, they arrange themselves into two choruses.

With this final scene, we have entered the realm of parody. The stage-directions make this clear at the outset and offer valuable clues as to how to interpret it: we are told that the two choruses of Gülleners are '*denen der griechischen Tragödien angenähert, nicht zufällig, sondern als Standortbestimmung, als gäbe ein havariertes Schiff, wie abgetrieben, die letzten Signale*' (132). The stranded ship is of course Güllen, and this last chorus, as we shall see in a moment, is an obscene cry for help, a sort of Mayday.

The resemblance to the chorus of a Greek tragedy, then, is quite deliberate. The model for Dürrenmatt's parody is to be found in Friedrich Hölderlin's translation of Sophocles' *Antigone*. The 'Ode on Man' in Act II is a panegyric on human prowess which begins:

> CHOR DER THEBANISCHEN ALTEN:
> Ungeheuer ist viel. Doch nichts
> Ungeheuerer, als der Mensch.
> Denn der, über die Nacht
> Des Meers, wenn gegen den Winter wehet
> Der Südwind, fähret er aus
> In geflügelten sausenden Häusern.[5]

Many are Man's talents, the ode continues, lofty his thoughts and his achievements; only sickness and death remain untamed:

> Und die Red' und den luftigen
> Gedanken und städtebeherrschenden Stolz

---

5 F. Hölderlin, *Sämtliche Werke*, ed. F. Beissner (Stuttgart, 1952), V, 219f. Cf. Gilbert Murray's translation (London, 1941), 32: 'Wonders are many, but none there be/ So strange, so fell, as the Child of Man.' The Greek adjective deinoV (translated by Hölderlin as 'ungeheuer') means 'awesome', 'fearful', 'terrible'; or in the Sophocles passage referred to here, 'strange', 'wonderful', 'inspiring amazement and respect'.

hat erlernet er, und übelwohnender
Hügel feuchte Lüfte, und
Die unglücklichen zu fliehen, die Pfeile. Allbewandert,
Unbewandert. Zu nichts kommt er.
Der Toten künftigen Ort nur
Zu fliehen weiß er nicht,
Und die Flucht unbeholfener Seuchen
Zu überdenken.

Human endeavour and the freedom of the human will are commended here as the necessary driving forces behind all progress, intellectual and ethical as well as physical and social; but classical Man must operate within the constraints of a moral system governed by the gods and the law. Tragic conflict arises when an individual mortal challenges these constraints, and is resolved when he or she finally submits to them.

In Dürrenmatt's chorus, there is no longer any hint of this productive-destructive dialectic, this tension between Man and cosmos. The Gülleners speak not of the human spirit taming the elements or conquering the seas, but of the physical threats, most of them man-made, which beset them; of their former grinding poverty; and of their sacred cow, wealth:

CHOR I: *Ungeheuer ist viel*
Gewaltige Erdbeben
Feuerspeiende Berge, Fluten des Meeres
Kriege auch, Panzer durch Kornfelder rasselnd
Der sonnenhafte Pilz der Atombombe.
CHOR II: *Doch nichts ist ungeheurer als* die Armut
Die nämlich kennt kein Abenteuer
Trostlos umfängt sie das Menschengeschlecht
Reiht
Öde Tage an öden Tag....
CHOR I: Denn die Arbeitsplätze, die brotbringenden einst
Sind leer
CHOR II: Und die *sausenden* Züge meiden den Ort.
ALLE: Wohl uns
FRAU ILL: Denen ein freundlich Geschick
ALLE: dies alles wandte. (132f.)

Dürrenmatt's parodistic intent is evident from his imitation of Hölderlin's verse-form and his adoption of identical words and phrases (*italicised* above); although perhaps, given the banality of the subject-matter, we should speak more properly of travesty than parody.

As the Gülleners' chorus continues with a list of some of the material benefits they now enjoy ('Im neuen, grüngekachelten Operationssaal/ operiert freudig der Arzt'; 'Wohlbeschuht/ Schmaucht ein jeglicher besseres Kraut'), Claire Zachanassian, 'Die Wohltäterin'

(134), is carried off in her sedan-chair. In referring to her in the stage-directions as 'ein altes Götzenbild aus Stein,' Dürrenmatt has chosen his words carefully, for as the Golden Calf she is indeed one of those 'graven images' which the Second Commandment forbids us to worship.

Not God, but *a* god–Mammon–is invoked (with fitting irony, by the Clergyman) in the final, blasphemous, stanza of the Gülleners' chorus, as the curtain falls on their town:

> ALLE: Es bewahre uns aber
> DER PFARRER: Ein Gott
> ALLE: In stampfender, rollender Zeit
> DER BÜRGERMEISTER: Den Wohlstand
> ALLE: Bewahre die heiligen Güter uns, bewahre den Frieden
> Bewahre die Freiheit.
> Nacht bleibe fern
> Verdunkele nimmermehr unsere Stadt
> Die neuerstandene prächtige
> Damit wir das Glück glücklich genießen.

For the men and women of Güllen, night is certain to be unwelcome: not only the symbolic night of recession and poverty, but also the real night, a time for thought, a time for memories, a time when conscience troubles. And what of their 'sacred possessions'? Once the Gülleners set store by spiritual values and prided themselves on their cultural heritage, however flimsy and laughable it might have appeared to outsiders. Now they cherish only material prosperity; peace to safeguard that prosperity; and, so they say, freedom–but freedom, as we spectators know, has no place in this list, for such freedom as the Gülleners ever possessed is long since discarded and not recoverable. The people of Güllen belong, totally and irredeemably, to Claire Zachanassian and to her wealth.

Chapter Two

A tragicomedy for our times

Every single one of Dürrenmatt's plays bears a subtitle, most frequently simply 'Komödie'. Sometimes the subtitle also supplies a little information about the construction of the work or its genre, as for instance in the case of *Die Physiker:* 'Eine Komödie in zwei Akten.' On other occasions, the subtitle may introduce a whimsical note, as with that of *Romulus der Große,* 'Eine ungeschichtliche historische Komödie in vier Akten.' But *Der Besuch der alten Dame* is the only play by Dürrenmatt to have been dubbed 'Eine tragische Komödie', and it seems to me that the studied ambiguity of this subtitle reflects precisely the structure and execution of the plot, as well as the paradoxical nature of the dénouement. On the one hand *Der Besuch der alten Dame* is a tragedy, in that it culminates in the death of Ill; yet on the other, the play bristles with comic features, such as amusing dialogue, characters and situations. These, it could perhaps be argued, fall into the category of comic relief, a familiar feature of tragedy proper; but *Der Besuch der alten Dame* also, and crucially, meets an essential formal requirement of comedy by having a happy ending–albeit only for the Gülleners. Ill's tragedy is Güllen's comedy, and furthermore, comedy in this strict sense has the last word, in the form of the 'Welt-Happy-End' (132) of the final chorus.

As we have seen, *Der Besuch der alten Dame* is a disturbing play, much more so than Dürrenmatt's reputation as a somewhat lightweight writer of ingenious detective stories and entertaining comedies would appear to allow. It may therefore be instructive to look behind that reputation and take stock of the main premisses on which his writing is based.

As one who wrote for a living for almost the whole of his adult life, Dürrenmatt's prime consideration was always a practical one: that his plays should be capable of making money. He approached the craft of drama as a professional, not a dilettante, and was ever conscious of the overwhelming need to sell theatre tickets. 'Auf die Ware,' as he once remarked, 'kommt es an' (*WA 24*: 88), and he always insisted that his 'product' must be regarded as a commodity like any other, competing for the public's money alongside other commodities and other forms of entertainment, be they ballet, concerts, cinema, television or whatever.

Dürrenmatt the writer readily accepted the challenge of the market economy–'Geldverdienen ist ein schriftstellerisches Stimulans' (*WA 26*: 59)–because success in the market-place, without subventions and sponsorships, brings independence. This, for Dürrenmatt, was not simply financial independence at the cost of pandering to low public taste (although financial independence was also, of course, a vital factor); nor was it simply the independence to say whatever he chose, even though the epithet 'unbequem' (uncomfortable) which he earned early in his career did reflect the fact that the comic facade of his writings concealed many an acute insight or unpalatable home truth.

For Dürrenmatt, as for Brecht before him, the notion of theatre was inseparable from the notion of entertainment, but though the two dramatists' opinions would have differed in many respects over the secondary functions of the theatre, they would surely have agreed that the element of amusement, if a necessary, is not in itself a sufficient condition of good drama. As thinking playwrights, both took issue with a range of matters of contemporary concern as well as with larger, universal or philosophical questions. Possibly the greatest difference between Brecht and Dürrenmatt lay in the fact that the former's approach was essentially didactic and optimistic, very much in the tradition of that eighteenth-century drama which he so despised: he believed that epic theatre would instruct whilst entertaining, and that the auditorium would be filled with acquisitive students seized by 'die Lust am Lernen.'[6] Dürrenmatt was more shrewd and more sceptical about the dramatist's power to persuade. Being fully aware that there is nothing to be gained (in any sense) from preaching ethics to empty houses, he reasoned pragmatically that only when the dramatist has induced theatre-goers to plant their bottoms on his seats could he begin to work on their minds. Comedy was the means by which Dürrenmatt lured the public into the theatre, for 'Die Komödie ist eine Mausefalle, in die das Publikum immer wieder gerät und immer noch geraten wird' (*WA 24*: 64).

There are several reasons why Dürrenmatt made comedy his chosen medium, besides the obvious, that he was outstandingly good at it and that it brought in the customers. Perhaps the most important one had to do with two words to which he frequently resorted: 'darstellen', 'to portray or depict' and 'gestalten', 'to fashion or shape'. Both of these words, of course, belong to the terminology of art, and it is surely no coincidence that Dürrenmatt's plays are so visually striking, that so many of the key concepts and terms he used in discussing

6 Bertolt Brecht, 'Vergnügungstheater oder Lehrtheater?' *Schriften zum Theater: Über eine nichtaristotelische Dramatik* (Frankfurt am Main, 1957), 66.

drama were drawn from art criticism, and that his favourite pastime, indeed his lifelong ruling passion, was painting and drawing. Drama, he argued, is an applied art which essentially consists in transforming some aspect or view of reality, as perceived by the playwright, into a stage reality. Different epochs have confronted dramatists with different sorts of reality, and dramatists have resorted to a whole variety of methods of portraying them. As in painting, the possibilities of depicting reality on stage range all the way from the mimetic or painstakingly naturalistic through to the abstract; and drama, like painting, underwent its most radical change in direction following the invention of photography, at which point the centuries-old goal of representational art, to simulate reality, ceased to be interesting because it was no longer a challenge. The camera, as it were, gave rise to abstract painting.

As well as reflecting trends in art, drama responds to changes in society, to political developments and to the movement of ideas. Dürrenmatt drew attention time and time again to the vast scale and the amorphous nature of modern society, in contrast to past epochs in which populations were smaller and communities more cohesive, and he considered it a central part of his mission as a dramatist, 'die Welt zu formen, aus ihrer Bildlosigkeit ein Bild zu machen,... ihr ein Gesicht [zu geben]' (*WA 26*: 67), for it is through his interpretation, or his manipulative portrayal, of some aspect of the 'Rätsel, das wir Welt nennen' (*WA 26*: 69), that the playwright performs his function as mediator between reality and the theatre-goer.

Although there is no overt didacticism in Dürrenmatt's writing –rather the opposite, for his plays and stories contain at best only clues, never precise pointers to what he himself thought about the issues they raise–, this certainly does not mean that he aimed for objectivity or that he adopted a hands-off approach. He expected his audiences to think for themselves, but he also fashioned his stage-worlds (he called them 'Eigenwelten') with great care so as to slant their thinking in particular directions. He regarded comedy, with its anarchic, iconoclastic tradition, as the medium best suited to his brand of verbal and visual satire, and tragedy, with its connotations of high moral values, as the best vehicle for conveying the eternal dilemmas and the universal truths of human existence that so often confront his characters. But whereas comedy addresses the theatre-goer with an easy familiarity born of its tendency to draw on topical, ephemeral events for its subject-matter, the difficulty with tragedy is that it leans heavily for its material on certain archetypes and recurrent situations, and resides in a rarified atmosphere of ideas and ideals, remote from the modern theatre-goer's experience. Tragedy, moreover, presupposes an ordered, hierarchical world quite unlike the one which the modern audience inhabits. So in order to convey to his fellow-mortals some sense of the tragic, and thereby regain the high moral ground occupied by tragedy in its heyday, Dürrenmatt was obliged to resort to sleight-of-hand: theatre-goers will not pay money to be preached to, but they do like to be amused; so by exploiting the fun and the immediacy of comedy, by filtering his ideas through the medium of comedy, he could confront his audiences with the tragic experience before they realised what was happening to them. What is served up to them by this method will not be 'pure' or 'high', unadulterated tragedy, of course, but the nearest approximation possible in this day and age:

> Doch ist das Tragische immer noch möglich, auch wenn die reine Tragödie nicht mehr möglich ist. Wir können das Tragische aus der Komödie heraus erzielen, hervorbringen als einen schrecklichen Moment, als einen sich öffnenden Abgrund. (*WA 24*: 62f.)

But why should Dürrenmatt consider the tragic experience to be of value to anyone living in the latter part of the twentieth century anyway; and why did he consider it necessary to resort to trickery in order to convey that experience to his audiences?

We find the beginnings of an answer to the first question in the introductory chapter to one of Dürrenmatt's best-known stories, *Die Panne*. Here he characterises modern existence as unstructured and banal, the modern individual as lacking all sense of purpose or continuity, and with no overview of the factors which determine the nature and quality of life and death:

> Der Alltag eines jeden,... schlechtes Wetter und Konjunktur, Sorgen und Plagen,... doch ohne Zusammenhang mit dem Weltganzen, mit dem Ablauf der Dinge und Undinge, mit dem Abspulen der Notwendigkeit. Das Schicksal hat die Bühne verlassen, auf der gespielt wird, um hinter den Kulissen zu lauern,... im Vordergrund wird alles zum Unfall, die Krankheiten, die Krisen.... So droht kein Gott mehr, keine Gerechtigkeit, kein Fatum wie in der fünften Symphonie, sondern Verkehrsunfälle, Deichbrüche infolge Fehlkonstruktion, Explosion einer Atombombenfabrik, hervorgerufen durch einen zerstreuten Laboranten, falsch eingestellte Brutmaschinen. In diese Welt der Pannen führt unser Weg. (*WA 20*: 38f.)

Life and society today, Dürrenmatt argues, differ in several important respects from what he regards as the last-ever epoch capable of sustaining high tragedy, the age of Friedrich Schiller. Unlike our sprawling, chaotic modern society, the scale of late eighteenth-century German life was still compact enough for the individual to grasp, and structured enough to provide a sense of self; by contrast with the faceless bureaucracy we encounter in contemporary government, one knew the identities of one's rulers, and one knew one's own place within the social and political hierarchy.

> Das Drama Schillers setzt eine sichtbare Welt voraus, die echte Staatsaktion, wie ja auch die griechische Tragödie. Sichtbar in der Kunst ist das Überschaubare. Der heutige Staat ist jedoch unüberschaubar, anonym, bürokratisch geworden.... Die echten Repräsentanten fehlen, und die tragischen Helden sind ohne Namen.... Die Kunst dringt nur noch bis zu den Opfern vor,... die Mächtigen erreicht sie nicht mehr. Kreons Sekretäre erledigen den Fall Antigone. (*WA 24*: 59f.)

Gone now is the pyramidal society, with the monarch at its apex, upon which all high tragedy is modelled; and gone, too, is that notion of Providence, of God or of some such supreme authority, which endows tragedy with a sense of ultimate optimism and justice, no matter what dire fate may overtake its heroes and heroines in their short time on earth. Inevitably, then, Dürrenmatt's answer to the rhetorical question, 'Läßt sich die heutige Welt ... mit der Dramatik Schillers gestalten?' must be an emphatic 'No.'

> Schiller schrieb, wie er schrieb, weil die Welt, in der er lebte, sich noch in der Welt, die er schrieb, die er sich als Historiker erschuf, spiegeln konnte. Gerade noch. War doch Napoleon der letzte Held im alten Sinne. Die heutige Welt ... läßt sich schwerlich in der Form des geschichtlichen Dramas Schillers bewältigen, allein aus dem Grunde, weil wir keine tragischen Helden, sondern nur Tragödien vorfinden, die von Weltmetzgern inszeniert und von Hackmaschinen ausgeführt werden. Aus Hitler und Stalin lassen sich keine Wallensteine mehr machen. (*WA 24*: 59)

So here we have an answer to our second question: 'pure' tragedy, tragedy in unvarnished form, is not a viable medium through which to portray our modern existence. But what of our first question? What, if anything, does the tragic experience have to offer the contemporary theatre-goer, when the economic, social and political conditions which govern our lives are so very different from those prevailing when tragedy flourished? At first, Dürrenmatt appears to be saying, 'Nothing whatsoever.' On the contrary, comedy, which thrives on disorder, seems far better equipped to capture the shapelessness, the tumultuous tone of modern life, than does tragedy:

> Die Aufgabe der Kunst ... ist, Gestalt, Konkretes zu schaffen. Dies vermag vor allem die Komödie. Die Tragödie, als die gestrengste Kunstgattung, setzt eine gestaltete Welt voraus. Die Komödie ... eine ungestaltete, im Werden, im Umsturz begriffene, eine Welt, die am Zusammenpacken ist wie die unsrige. (*WA 24*: 61)

And furthermore: tragedy encourages empathy and identification with the hero on the part of the spectator, an emotional, uncritical stance already roundly criticised by Brecht. Tragedy brings its characters and its audiences into myopically close proximity to one another, which results in an unfocussed view of the issues at stake, whereas 'Die Komödie schafft Distanz' (*WA 24*: 61): comedy, by making us take a step backwards–by, in a sense, alienating us–puts matters into proper perspective and allows us to perceive them with a degree of objectivity. Elsewhere, indeed, Dürrenmatt asserts that comedy, rather than epic theatre, is the theatre of non-identification *par excellence*:

> Das Komische tritt nur ein, wo wir objektivieren, das heißt, wo wir eine Gestalt oder eine Handlung als Ganzes überblicken, was nur möglich ist, wo wir Distanz bewahren.... Das Komische muß uns nicht nahe gehen wie das Tragische, um auf uns zu wirken, das Komische wirkt auf uns, weil wir von ihm Abstand nehmen, unser Gelächter ist die Kraft, die den komischen Gegenstand von uns wegtreibt. (*Dramaturgische Überlegungen zu den 'Wiedertäufern'*, *WA 10*: 132)

Yet there is also another consideration, another way of focussing on a tangible object in our world of bewildering abstractions: we can still find a sense of purpose, as well as general rules for living–moral guidance, truth and justice–in examples set by specific individuals: 'Es ist immer noch möglich, den mutigen Menschen zu zeigen.... Die verlorene Weltordnung wird in ihrer Brust wieder hergestellt, das Allgemeine entgeht meinem Zugriff' (*WA 24*: 63). And even in a world in which no one ever seems prepared to take the blame when things go wrong, we can still witness, on stage at least, that shouldering of personal responsibility which is the hallmark of the tragic experience, even though tragedy in the strict sense is denied us.

Without the social structures and frequently without the religious support available to past generations, each one of us today has to find our own way of coping with life: every man, to misquote John Donne now, is an island, entire of itself, and there can be no general, universal recipe for living–only a series of individual grapplings with the myriad problems and dilemmas of existence:

> Die Chance liegt allein noch beim Einzelnen. Der Einzelne hat die Welt zu bestehen. Von ihm aus ist alles wieder zu gewinnen. Nur von ihm, das ist seine grausame Einschränkung. Der Schriftsteller gebe es auf, die Welt retten zu wollen. Er wage es wieder, die Welt zu formen, aus ihrer Bildlosigkeit ein Bild zu machen. (*WA 26*: 67)

These words bring us back full circle to our starting-point in this discussion, the dramatist's urge to 'give the world a face.' We can heighten our awareness of ourselves as unique individuals, as well as draw moral strength, from the experiences of Dürrenmatt's latter-day heroes, his 'mutige Menschen'; but only if we can observe them functioning in a convincing and coherent context, one which is both appropriate to the quasi-tragic nature of their circumstances and organised in a form and on a scale we find psychologically manageable. Achieving this is no mean task, and calls, as we saw, for subterfuge, for 'Die Tragödie ... setzt eine Gemeinschaft voraus, die heute nicht immer ohne Peinlichkeit als vorhanden fingiert werden kann' (*WA 24*: 64). Hence Dürrenmatt has no scruples whatsoever about resorting to the 'mousetrap' of comedy, both initially as the means of exposing his audience to the tragic experience, and subsequently as the means of modulating their responses to the plight of the hero in such a way as to preclude the facile, self-congratulatory identification which was central to the 'Aristotelean theatre' so vehemently attacked by Brecht.

How, then, is an amorphous group of modern spectators to be moulded, or one should perhaps say 'softened up', for their part in the stage tragedy which awaits them? Since the tragic experience, like all theatre, is a communal act, Dürrenmatt goes to considerable lengths in *Der Besuch der alten Dame* to create a specific community with a clearly delineated identity–a 'Gemeinschaft' of the type he finds so little in evidence in our modern world–and to involve his audience in the affairs of that community; for (to adapt slightly the passage quoted a moment ago) 'die Tragödie muß uns nahe gehen, um auf uns zu wirken.' Curiously–or so it seems at first sight–, he locates just such a community in the parish-pump setting he knows so intimately from his childhood: Güllen, for all its pretensions to be something grander, is nothing but an overgrown village, and its inhabitants, more importantly, display all the attributes of people who know one another's affairs and circumstances only too well. One drama critic recalls a remark of Dürrenmatt's which bears directly on this subject:

> Dürrenmatt erklärte mir einmal ..., er schreibe lauter Dorfgeschichten, er sei im Grunde ein Dorfpoet.... Nun, einst waren Theben, Mykene, Argos und Troja nicht größer, als man sich Güllen vorstellt. Man spaziere nur einmal rund um Troja. In diesem Sinn schrieben auch die antiken Tragiker Dorfgeschichten.[7]

Complementary to the use Dürrenmatt makes of the Greek chorus in *Der Besuch der alten Dame*, then, is his choice of setting, based on a social model that is both completely familiar to him and similar in scale to the ancient Greek society he seeks to emulate. It has to be admitted, of course, that even if the two communities of Güllen and,

7 Wolfgang Kraus, *Programmheft* des Schauspielhauses Zürich, June 1977, 19f.

say, ancient Thebes resemble one another in size, it is not immediately apparent that any of the other significant elements such as, say, the cultural atmosphere or the ethical climate have much in common with one another; which is why Dürrenmatt, as we saw in the textual commentary section, takes so much trouble to establish links between Güllen and classical Greece, not only by his use of the chorus, but also by making the Teacher liken Claire to 'eine griechische Schicksalsgöttin', 'eine Parze', and so on, and ultimately by turning Ill into a figure worthy to join the ranks of the classical heroes.

But if the members of Dürrenmatt's audience do not immediately see the intended connection between Güllen and the world of Greek tragedy, they are more than likely (especially if they are a Swiss audience) to recognise the men and women of Güllen. In a Swiss village, people are associated with and indeed identified by their calling or post: hence 'der Bürgermeister', 'der Polizist', etc. This form of stereotyping, and the associated practice of allocating each member of the community to a particular point on the social scale is, as we remarked earlier, an authentic feature of village life, and one which Dürrenmatt, as a child of the manse, knows only too well; for apart from the leader of the parish council, the three most important people in village society, each of whom enjoys a special position because of his calling and his superior education, are the teacher, the doctor and the clergyman.

The only truly individual Güllener is Ill, and at first even he is labelled (as the Grocer, as the Next Mayor and as Claire's Former Sweetheart), before he begins to break free of the group and establish his own identity, and with it his own isolation, in Act III.

It should not, however, be supposed in the case of *Der Besuch der alten Dame* that being type-cast is synonymous, as it is with the characters in certain forms of comedy, with being caricatures. Rather, the very fact that they are stereotypes makes the people of Güllen into representative figures who together add up to a plausible social unit with all the important elements in place. And because the inhabitants of Güllen are just ordinary people in familiar professions, the spectators will be inclined to identify with them, a fact which becomes increasingly disturbing for the audience as the play progresses and which some productions have exploited to the full by making the spectators join in with the Gülleners, reading a placard aloud, in the oath-swearing ceremony which precedes Ill's death. This process of initial identification followed by eventual distancing is precisely what Dürrenmatt intends, in line with his reception theory of tragedy: the spectator at first empathises with the hero, only to retreat when it becomes apparent that the hero is going to die, and furthermore, to die on behalf of or even *instead of* the spectator. Both aspects–the notion of the scapegoat or sacrificial lamb and the sentiment that 'There but for the grace of God go I'–are psychologically and historically fundamental to tragedy, this so highly stylised art form which seems to have had its beginnings in the sacrifices–whether human or animal–performed by communities in ancient times so as to ensure good harvests.[8]

According to one theory on the origins of tragedy, a young man was selected to represent his community as Corn King in a fertility rite which entailed his being granted royal or quasi-royal status for a fixed term, at the end of which he was taken out and ceremonially slaughtered and his blood sprinkled on the fields as an offering to the crop deity; his successor was then chosen and would be similarly slaughtered in due course. With the passage of time, the death of the scapegoat–for such he was–came to be associated with the general well-being of the community, rather than specifically with the quality of the harvest; but the principles remained the same: the sacrifice was still a 'King', so that he would embody the best the community had to offer; he would suffer (the more, the better: for the quality of his suffering determined the quality of the offering, as well as the degree of 'atonement' the community could buy with his death); he would die 'for'–on behalf of, and in place of–his fellows; and with his dispatch the community, its debts to the gods paid off for a time, could emerge rejuvenated and ready to embark on a fresh cycle.

As society progressed, human sacrifices were abandoned and the focus of attention shifted from purely materialistic considerations to ethical and religious ones. At this point tragedy began to emerge as an art form with, as its central event, the death of the 'noble' hero, a sublimated version of the sacrifice proper. In place of being blessed with plentiful harvests, the community–or, as it had by now become, the audience–experienced the moral cleansing and rebirth known in tragic theory as *catharsis*. But in this more advanced, sophisticated society governed by morality rather than expediency, the hero who died had to be more than a mere victim, though he was that, too. The death of a human being was now unacceptable unless it could be in some way justified as stemming from his own make-up or conduct: hence the idea in tragedy of *hamartia* ('error of judgement') and its concomitant, *hybris* ('overweening pride'). Geoffrey Brereton describes the nature and role of the tragic hero, and the complex

8 See Geoffrey Brereton, *Principles of Tragedy* (London, 1968), 48f. The Old Testament Book of Leviticus lays down a complex set of laws governing the ritual slaughter of bullocks, lambs and the like, to meet a variety of contingencies ranging from peace offerings to procedures for the cleansing of lepers; and also provides for a communal cleansing from sin through the scapegoat, on whose head 'all the iniquities of the children of Israel, and all their transgressions in all their sins' are heaped (16: 21).

mechanism which enables his character and actions to be regarded on the one hand as personal attributes, yet simultaneously as representative of and deriving from the group to which he belongs:

> The transgressions of the community are transferred symbolically to the sacrificial King, who goes to his death loaded with both excellence and sin, with the shame of the community as well as its pride.... The King, representing the 'best' qualities of the community, can at the same time be made responsible for its worst qualities, be at once hero and scapegoat. Is not this, it may be asked, the essence of the tragic ambivalence; a definition, in general terms, of the typical tragic hero? (*Principles of Tragedy*, 49f.)

And is not this also, we may ask in turn, the essence of Ill's situation? For he too emerges from mediocrity into the limelight, is found guilty of a crime, but presently rises above his fellows and above his former self; and when he finally dies, he does so in order to pay for something larger than the crime he has himself committed, so that the townspeople may enjoy a 'better' life.

But of course the events which overtake the tragic hero concern not only the community to which he belongs, but also, and crucially, his own person. The spectators witness a process in which his standing in society increases dramatically, only to take an equally sensational downturn which culminates in disaster and death; but such is the ambivalence of tragedy that the hero's moral stature grows in inverse proportion to his material decline so that, at the end, he towers high above everyone around him. This is precisely what happens in *Der Besuch der alten Dame*, with Ill's death a moral victory for him and a moral capitulation for his fellow-citizens. In accepting death as the proper penalty for his misdeeds of long ago, Ill acknowledges the absolute justice of Claire's demands, irrespective of the limitations of conventional justice; and his act of justice not only balances off against the issues which gave rise to it, but paradoxically also elevates him above them, attaining for him something akin to true heroic status. In going to his death, Ill demonstrates that courage and independence which earn for him the ultimate Dürrenmattian accolade, that of being 'ein mutiger Mensch'.

Naturally, Ill's heroism can only rank as a personal achievement, not as an exhortation to the theatre-going public to follow suit. But whereas high tragedy is able to suggest general, demonstrative inferences by presuming a seamless continuum between the moral considerations which lead to the hero's death and the ethical precepts prevailing within the community at large, no such correspondence exists in *Der Besuch der alten Dame*. Instead of being morally uplifted by Ill's death, the Gülleners benefit only materially. The irony is, first, that they greet the arrival of material prosperity (in the parodistic final Chorus) in terms better suited to things of the spirit than things of the flesh; and secondly, that the plot of *Der Besuch der alten Dame* constitutes not only a chilling exposure of the hypocrisy of the Gülleners, but also a clever reversion as regards the history of tragedy as a genre, whereby Dürrenmatt dismantles the facade of morality which civilised society has erected around tragedy in order to expose the crude self-interest in which it is founded. Ill, in other words, is none other than the Corn King come again.

Nor is the irony lost on Dürrenmatt's audiences. Having once identified with them, we cannot escape recognising ourselves in the people of Güllen as they embrace Mammon with open arms, and we cannot help squirming as we witness ourselves, or people just like us, abandoning what principles we had as we succumb to the siren call of consumerism. True to Dürrenmatt's intention, our instinctive efforts to distance ourselves from the Gülleners, once we begin to realise where identification is leading us, serve only to intensify our discomfort, for the effect of whatever distance we are able to attain is not to set us apart from the goings-on on stage, as we would surely wish, but rather to give us a more sharply focussed, and therefore more acutely painful, view of these events, and by extension of our own circumstances.

The apparent contradiction between my claim, that the experience of tragedy creates distance, and Dürrenmatt's assertion that 'Die Komödie schafft Distanz', can, I hope, be explained and resolved. Comedy does indeed encourage the spectator to distance himself from the characters and events on stage, and the more mocking or satirical the humour, the greater the gulf: we laugh at a pompous man who slips on a banana skin partly because we enjoy the injury sustained by his self-importance, but partly also out of a feeling of relief and superiority that we ourselves have not been so unfortunate. In other words, we distance ourselves from his predicament. Dürrenmatt argues similarly, in the postscript to *Die Wiedertäufer*, that the clown is the isolated individual *par excellence*, the person everyone laughs *at*, rather than *with* (*WA 10*: 132).

Tragedy, on the other hand, begins by engendering sympathy and identification, but later, as we saw, it forces the spectator to try (unsuccessfully) to wriggle free of the ties which bind him to the hero. Lured by the comic bait of laughing at someone else's discomfiture, we find ourselves pinned helplessly in the identification trap of tragedy. True to his dictum that 'Die Tragödie und die Komödie sind Formbegriffe,... die Gleiches zu umschreiben vermögen' (*WA 24*: 62), Dürrenmatt's unique blend of the comic and the tragic yields up a productive tension which is sustained throughout the play and culminates for the spectator in something very close to the experience of tragedy proper.

Yet in two important respects the fate of Ill and its impact on his fellow-Gülleners may possibly fall short of the truly tragic: as regards the justice, and as regards the necessity, of Ill's death. As far as the first of these is concerned, we might wonder whether Ill pays a disproportionately high price for his youthful crime: any hint of unfairness runs counter to the spirit of tragedy, whereby everyone must be seen to get his just deserts, and even though Ill himself fully accepts his punishment, it may perhaps be felt by some spectators that what Claire is demanding is *absolute* retribution (as opposed to justice) as compensation for the *relatively* impaired quality of the life she has led. What is more, her imperious handling of her fellow-mortals grotesquely mars the tragedy of Ill's death: in manipulating people and events so as to convey an air of divinity when she is after all only human, she gravely strains the rationale behind his acceptance of the terms she lays down. That is, Ill's death is rendered untragic to the extent that he mistakes Claire's all-too-human demand for vengeance for the altogether higher principle of justice.

The matter of necessity is also of some significance in tragedy, and here, too, one feels that the conditions have not been fully satisfied. Tragic necessity (*Notwendigkeit* or, less frequently, *Not*) is the acknowledgement by all concerned, players and spectators alike, of the inevitability of the hero's death. Dürrenmatt recognises its prime importance within the tragic scheme of things when he observes in *Theaterprobleme*: 'Die Tragödie setzt Schuld, Not, Maß, Übersicht, Verantwortung voraus' (*WA 24*: 62). It is essential that tragic necessity should be well founded in plot, character and circumstance if it is to carry conviction. The difficulty in the case of *Der Besuch der alten Dame* is that, although the material hardship of the Gülleners is admittedly considerable, it is not so severe as to be compelling. Certainly Güllen is poor by comparison with the neighbouring towns, but its poverty is still only relative: as the Mayor says in another context, 'Noch sind wir in Europa' (50), and the issue confronting the people of Güllen is not about, say, survival in a third-world situation, but rather, about whether they can afford an expensive brand of cigarettes or have to make do with cheaper ones. That being so, it is impossible to uphold the notion of tragic necessity as applying to the Gülleners, and they stand revealed in all their shallowness in the oath-swearing ceremony which precedes Ill's death, when they accept Claire's proposition 'Nicht des Geldes ... sondern der Gerechtigkeit wegen ... und aus Gewissensnot' (124).

(The ambiguity of the term *Gewissensnot* serves merely to reinforce the point, since it means not only 'moral dilemma', as they intend, but also 'lack or poverty of conscience', which they do not). All in all, then, and despite Dürrenmatt's careful efforts, the tragic atmosphere cannot ultimately be sustained, or even fully realised, in Güllen. Indeed in Dürrenmatt's own judgement, '[Ills] Tod ist sinnvoll und sinnlos zugleich. Sinnvoll allein wäre er im mythischen Reich einer antiken Polis, nun spielt sich die Geschichte in Güllen ab. In der Gegenwart' (143).

Dürrenmatt was a highly provocative writer, and there have been many attempts to label him, ranging from the clinical ('a merciless observer') to the sensational ('ein literarischer Raketenfabrikant').[9] But one of the most apt descriptions of his attitude to the human condition and how it influenced his activities as a writer came from his own lips, when he described himself, in a televised documentary conducted by his second wife, Charlotte Kerr, as 'ein Diagnostiker.'[10] As I have emphasised, his primary function, with *Der Besuch der alten Dame* as with every one of his works of drama or fiction, was to entertain, but identifying the problems and dilemmas of modern life, or rather enabling us to identify them for ourselves, invariably came a very close second. His hope, it seems to me, was that by the examples he set before us we might see for ourselves not only the evils of the society in which we live, but also the possibility of righting some of those evils and, even more importantly, of asserting our own independence and realising our own potential amidst the facelessness of late twentieth-century existence. For whatever we may feel about the senselessness or otherwise of Ill's death, he is to be commended for summoning up the courage to act according to his own lights; and surely, Dürrenmatt urges us, each one of us can make the effort to do the same?

9 Martin Esslin, *Plays and Players*, 10 (1963), 15f.; Siegfried M. Pistorius, 'Der Einsiedler von Neuchâtel. Besuch bei Friedrich Dürrenmatt,' *Westfälische Rundschau*, 19.2.59.

10 *Portrait eines Planeten, mit Friedrich Dürrenmatt. Ein Film von Charlotte Kerr* (Stuttgart, 1984).

Chapter Three

The story behind the play

Der Besuch der alten Dame owes much of its huge success to its originality and ingenuity of plot, and this study would be incomplete if it were to conclude without giving some consideration to at least the key features which together make this play so unique.

I consider that Dürrenmatt's three most important decisions, as regards the composition of *Der Besuch der alten Dame*, were: setting his tragicomedy of revenge in a small township, where all the citizens know–or think they know–one another; choosing a woman for the central role; and making her arrive in Güllen in the way that she does. The play owes a very great deal to these decisions, for together they are responsible for the impact of the opening scenes and subsequently also for the uniquely compelling direction taken by the plot. It may therefore be instructive to examine each of these decisions in turn.

We have already noted Dürrenmatt's views on the merits of a small community like Güllen when it comes to recapturing the mood of classical tragedy in the modern world. But the Güllen on which the opening curtain rises is also, in stage terms, the classic territory of the interloper, that alien figure who bursts into the midst of an established social group with explosive, and hence highly dramatic, consequences. Apparently close-knit, but in reality held together only by the loose bonds of shared adversity, the hermetic, inward-looking community of Güllen is a powder-keg waiting to be blown sky-high by a destructive outsider in the shape of Claire Zachanassian.

The Gülleners are indeed doubly vulnerable, for besides their susceptibility to seduction by the prospect of great wealth, there is the fact that their guard is down to Claire: having conveniently forgotten the truth about Kläri Wäscher for the best part of a lifetime, they delude themselves that she is one of them and sure to be nostalgic and bountiful. Dürrenmatt also deludes us, the spectators, by means of the Gülleners' dialogue in the first scene and also by the very title of the play: old ladies are gentle, kindly souls; a little delicate, perhaps, but that only adds to their charm; and bound to be romantically inclined, especially when a homecoming after forty-five years' absence is involved. Like the Gülleners, we expect nothing but generosity from their visitor. If Dürrenmatt's first stroke of genius, then, was to spot the dramatic potential of a community so close to his own experience, his second was to recognise and exploit our prejudices about gender. Let us now consider more closely how he does this.

We are more fortunate than the early critics of *Der Besuch der alten Dame*, for since the publication of *Stoffe I-III* in 1981 we have been able to trace with some accuracy the evolution of the plot *en route* to becoming a stage production. The prototype of *Der Besuch der alten Dame* is a short story entitled *Mondfinsternis*, in which a man returns after forty years in Canada to his native village perched high in the Alps. Walt Locher (or Lotcher, as he is known in the Anglo-Saxon world) is a veritable colossus, with a huge appetite for women and drink, and immensely rich. Discovering that his ex-lover, Kläri (whom he had completely forgotten about in the interim), is now married to an old rival, Lotcher casually announces that he will give fourteen million to the villagers, one million for each family. He has the money with him in cash, in a suitcase in his car. The only condition is that they kill Kläri's husband, Döufu Mani. With that he instals himself upstairs in the village inn with a plentiful supply of girls and schnaps and waits. The innkeeper, who is also the Mayor, makes no more than a token attempt to reject Lotcher's proposition. Indeed, although he announces that he will first have to convene a meeting of the villagers and that they will surely decline, he has already implicitly accepted on their behalf by trying to talk Lotcher into increasing his offer to thirty million; and he spends the next ten days encouraging all the girls in the village to sleep with Lotcher whilst he eagerly counts the money in the case.

Discussion among the men attending the meeting to consider Lotcher's offer is perfunctory and mainly conducted at the level of personal abuse; only one old peasant is against murdering Mani, and he is quickly silenced by the threat of his incestuous relations with his daughter and grand-daughter being reported to the authorities. Fortunately, the victim, Mani, announces that he is quite willing to be killed: he realises how badly the village needs the money, and in any case life is no joy any longer; the best thing would be for them to get it over with straight away. But Lotcher insists that they must wait for the next full moon in ten days' time.

We are given no indication of how Mani spends the waiting time, except that a watch is kept on him, lest he should change his mind; and that the village policeman, an incomer and therefore not privy to what is going on, is plied liberally with drink. Certainly we are given no hint of any emotional build-up in the victim's mind. He has only one request, to visit the agricultural show in the city the day before his execution, so that he will be able to advise his two sons on how best to spend their new-found wealth on farming equipment.

Sadly, however, Mani learns just before going to his death that his sacrifice will be completely in vain. His elder son (who in fact is really Lotcher's) reproaches him for marrying his mother: had Mani only left her alone, so he believes, his proper father would have married her and he would have been a rich Canadian by now. He will take the money and go there, and he has no intention of sharing it with his half-brother.

Frau Mani, on the other hand, will have nothing to do with the money. She knows that her husband, although misguided, is a decent man, and sees that Lotcher is only out for mischief:

> Er ist nicht gekommen, um sich an dir zu rächen, wie du dir wahrscheinlich einbildest, er will sich einen Spaß mit uns armen Menschen erlauben, weil er uns verachtet, heute und damals. Und auch unser Schicksal amüsiert ihn: die im Dorf werden untereinander Streit bekommen,... in diesem Dorf wird es wie in der Hölle zugehen, wenn sie dich erschlagen haben, alle möchten dann über einander herfallen wie die Wölfe, und es doch nicht wagen, aus Angst, jemand werde reden. (*Stoffe I-III*, 286f.)

The villagers have agreed that, in order to make Mani's death look like an accident, he should be struck by a falling tree. Since peasants are nothing if not practical, they decide on a large beech tree which can later provide the long-promised new roof timbers for the church (thereby, incidentally, implicating the unsuspecting Clergyman). The actual execution has a strong element of clumsy farce about it. The appointed tree has been partly sawn through in advance. Mani sits down at the foot of it and waits for his fellow-villagers, chopping in unison, to bring it down on top of him. Unfortunately, this takes longer than expected, and in the midst of it they witness an eclipse of the moon. This would have been Mani's opportunity to escape, but he sits motionless whilst the others, superstitious peasants to a man, fall down on their knees and pray. At last, the eclipse over, they resume their chopping and Mani lies 'schön zerquetscht,... ein einziger Brei' (*Stoffe I-III*, 292), in the gentle, soothing, silvery light of the full moon.

Lotcher now departs in his Cadillac, leaving behind the suitcase full of notes. On the way down he meets Kläri, who is also leaving the village. From their first conversation in forty years, we learn that Lotcher had been unaware, before he entered the inn that night, that Kläri had been expecting his child when he left for Canada; that he had returned to his native village, not to seek revenge, but 'aus Gutmütigkeit wahrscheinlich. Um euch etwas auf die Beine zu bringen, was sind schon vierzehn Millionen' (*Stoffe I-III*, 296); and that his call for Mani's death had only been a sudden whim, the spur-of-the moment impulse of an ageing man in response to an overwhelming urge to live his life all over again: 'will man leben, will man auch morden' (*Stoffe I-III*, 297). We have been deeply shaken by the callousness of the villagers and by their victim's fatalism; now we are struck by Lotcher's utter casualness and hence the complete lack of purpose behind Mani's death. In Lotcher's words it was, like his many conquests, 'immaterial':

> Wer alles in diesen zehn Tagen da oben in meinem Bett gelegen hat, um sich einen oder mehrere Tausenderscheine zu holen, ist mir gleichgültig, so wie es mir gleichgültig ist, wen sie totgeschlagen haben. Es hätte auch ein anderer sein können als Mani, ich habe die Leiche nicht angeschaut, und wenn sie niemanden totgeschlagen hätten, hätte ich ihnen das Geld auch gegeben.

Kläri continues down on foot to catch her slow train out of the valley; Lotcher succumbs shortly afterwards to a heart-attack; and by way of a final irony, the federal authorities choose this moment to rescue the benighted village from its backwardness by a huge injection of cash, thus rendering their act of murder for gain more pointless still.

Several interesting details emerge from a comparison of *Mondfinsternis* with the reworked version. There are, of course, a number of obvious points of resemblance, such as the homecoming of the central character to a small, inward-looking, impoverished community after a long absence, the irresistible offer of vast wealth and the death of a victim in exchange for prosperity. Then again, some elements have been retained in the later version, but altered: in both stories, for example, we encounter a Policeman, a Clergyman and a Teacher, but in *Mondfinsternis* all three, being incomers, are kept ignorant of what is happening, whereas in *Der Besuch der alten Dame* they are integral and indeed important members of the community and closely involved with the events surrounding Ill's death. The *Gemeindeversammlung* convened to discuss Lotcher's offer has no direct equivalent in *Der Besuch der alten Dame*, but the banquet held in Claire's honour, at which she puts her proposition to the Gülleners, corresponds to such a gathering, albeit in a modified form which allows for the element of surprise desired by the playwright.

But by far the most significant differences between *Mondfinsternis* and *Der Besuch der alten Dame* concern Dürrenmatt's treatment of the sexes. In the first place, obviously, the male central character of the story has become the eponymous female protagonist of the play. In *Stoffe I-III*, Dürrenmatt explains in some detail how this change came about. In 1954, with his wife ill in hospital, he started to work again on his original draft of *Mondfinsternis*, but then, as he was heavily in debt, decided that there was more chance of making money out of the story as a play than as a piece of prose. Dürrenmatt was fond of narrating, as he does here, how the idea for the opening scene came to him one day in a flash. He was travelling back and forth regularly between his home in Neuchâtel and Bern, where his wife was being treated. The expresses on this route stop at two tiny stations, Ins and Kerzers, 'wodurch man gezwungen ist, die beiden kleinen trostlosen Bahnhöfe zu betrachten, ungeduldig über den Unterbruch, wenn er auch nur eine, zwei Minuten dauert' (*Stoffe I-III*, 248). As we saw at the beginning of this study, being able to boast a station confers a certain status on a Swiss community. This accounts for the elevation of the mountain village setting of *Mondfinsternis* to a township in the play–though this of course is a distinction which Güllen in its decline has lost, and until the day when Claire brings the express to an abrupt halt, only local trains (*Personenzüge*) stop there.

Putting a railway station on the stage, Dürrenmatt continues, calls for improvisation: the townspeople sitting on the platform swivel their heads to indicate a passing train, etc. But waiting for a train to arrive also creates tension, one of the most valuable tools available to a dramatist. If the visitor is so important that the entire town has turned out, the tension rises, and if he or she arrives sooner than expected, or is delayed, the tension is heightened even more. As we know, Dürrenmatt chose 'sooner', and he further emphasised the immense power and the exotic nature of Claire Zachanassian by her weird retinue and her bizarre habit of travelling everywhere in a sedan-chair; but he first demonstrated that she was a law unto herself by making her stop the hurtling express by means of the emergency brake: no self-respecting Swiss citizen would ever dream of interfering with that most sacred of institutions, the railway.

The sort of person who steps off that train, so Dürrenmatt argues–and here he becomes somewhat less incisive and less convincing–must be a woman. Contrary to his statements on other occasions, he maintains here that the part of Claire Zachanassian was not written with a particular actress, Therese Giehse, in mind, but evolved naturally from the considerations outlined above: 'Diese neuen Prämissen, zu denen noch viele andere kamen, gaben schließlich den Ausschlag –"bühnenatmosphärisch" gleichsam–zur Geschlechtsänderung, nicht der Wunsch, für die Giehse eine Rolle zu schreiben' (*Stoffe I-III*, 294).[11]

---

11 *Der Besuch der alten Dame* was the first Dürrenmatt play in which Therese Giehse appeared; by 1956, however, she was at the height of a distinguished career which had begun in Munich in the twenties and continued in exile, from 1933, at the *Schauspielhaus*, Zürich. She was a good friend of Dürrenmatt's. He told me, when I visited him in Neuchâtel in 1986, that she inquired one day, 'Warum schreibst du keine guten Rollen für Frauen?' and that this inspired him to invent the character of Claire Zachanassian; certainly this was the first of three consecutive roles for Therese Giehse as leading lady in Dürrenmatt plays, the others being as

Continued/

Dürrenmatt is insistent: 'Erzwingt die erste Szene des *Besuchs der alten Dame* eine Frau, erzwingt der Beginn der *Mondfinsternis* einen Mann; da wird niemand erwartet, sondern es dringt einer ein, und der Einzelne, der da eindringt, kann nur allein kommen.' Certainly with his aggressive sexuality, alluded to here by the term 'eindringen' (which implies 'intrusion', but also 'thrusting' or 'penetration'), Walt Lotcher could only be male. But whether or not arbitrary callousness is a male characteristic, and a long memory for past hurt is more in keeping with the female temperament, is rather moot; as is the question of whether a death caused by casual whim is particularly a male crime any more than one brought about by life-long scheming for revenge is a female one.

The minor characters have also undergone changes on the sexual front in the course of converting the short story into a drama. The main difference between *Mondfinsternis* and *Der Besuch der alten Dame* is that in the former, gender stereotyping is much more marked. In the story, the role of women is clearly and narrowly defined: they exist for sex, for bearing children and as a source of manual labour; in the play, on the other hand, the minor female characters are scarcely differentiated from the males: in the face of Claire's dominance, the townspeople largely lose their identity, including their sexual identity, so that it is immaterial, for instance, whether the customers in Ill's shop are men or women. The men of the story spend all of their free time in the village inn, drinking and playing cards; in this respect they are not very different from the men lounging on the station platform in *Der Besuch der alten Dame*. But one important function remains a male preserve in both versions of the tale: the communal act of taking and carrying out decisions. By reserving Ill's and Mani's executions exclusively for the menfolk, Dürrenmatt emphasises the primitive, ritualistic, atavistic nature of the circumstances surrounding their deaths. The effect is rendered the more spine-chilling in *Der Besuch der alten Dame* by the Gülleners' frequent protestations that they are civilised people, whereas in *Mondfinsternis* we are given the impression that the peasants in question cannot help being ignorant, brutal and unfeeling, and the pragmatic manner of all concerned (the victim included) effectively blunts our responses to Mani's murder.

We are also prevented from taking Mani's death too seriously by the farcical manner of his dying and by his own almost bovine acquiescence. By contrast, Ill, though by no means an intellectual, denies,

---

Ottilie Frank (*Frank der Fünfte*, 1959) and Fräulein Doktor Mathilde von Zahnd (*Die Physiker*, 1962).

challenges and finally comes to terms with the inevitability and the justice of his death in a process which both raises the moral tone of the plot and elevates him to the status of a tragic hero, so that by transcending himself he becomes at last a man of courage, 'ein mutiger Mensch'.[12]

12 See *Theaterprobleme*, *WA 24*: 63. In Dürrenmatt's later terminology (following the publication of *Der Mitmacher. Ein Komplex* in 1976), a character such as Ill would be termed 'ein ironischer Held': 'ironisch' because he is able to achieve 'Distanz' from himself, stepping outside his own subjectivity and viewing himself and his situation in a broader perspective.

Conclusion

Der Besuch der alten Dame is truly a morality play for our acquisitive society: indeed, it was originally subtitled, pointedly, 'Komödie der Hochkonjunktur'. It bears, directly and uncomfortably, on such evergreen issues as the dividing line between individual and collective responsibility, but also on aspects of modern life in particular, such as the uneasy tension between affluence and ethical conduct.

Dürrenmatt's highly original, entertaining yet deeply shocking contribution to the contemporary debate about materialism is to subvert and pervert an art form conventionally associated with the highest ethical values so as to accommodate those basest of sentiments and motives, fear and greed. And because we are in the realms of tragicomedy and parody here, rather than pure tragedy, the audience is denied the ultimate comfort of *catharsis*: we go home chastened, not uplifted, by Ill's death.

Yet he evidently believed, and demonstrated beyond doubt in *Der Besuch der alten Dame*, that there is still room for single acts of courage and moral behaviour, both on and off the stage; that such acts represent the assertion of decency and freedom in the face of the grasping and the levelling, de-humanising processes at work in modern society; and that by depicting such acts he could convey to audiences unschooled in the conventions of tragedy something of the tragic experience. As in the present instance, the dramatist could employ his skill to give us insights into issues or dilemmas and even indicate possible responses; but, since he respected the individual's freedom of choice above all else, he could never compel us to respond in a particular way: 'Die Dramatik kann den Zuschauer überlisten, sich der Wirklichkeit auszusetzen, aber nicht zwingen, ihr standzuhalten oder sie gar zu bewältigen' (*21 Punkte zu den 'Physikern,' WA 7*: 93). He might show us examples of certain types of behaviour and their consequences, but in the end we must each work out our own principles and our own destinies, for 'Nur im Privaten kann die Welt auch heute noch in Ordnung sein.'[13]

---

13 Dürrenmatt, *Ansprache anläßlich der Verleihung des Kriegsblinden-Preises* (1957), *Theater-Schriften und Reden* (Zürich, 1966), 48.

Postscript

Friedrich Dürrenmatt died suddenly at his home in Neuchâtel on the night of Friday 14th December, 1990, just three weeks away from his seventieth birthday. Elaborate preparations were being made by his many friends and associates to celebrate this landmark in the life of Switzerland's outstanding man of letters, even though the man himself, with characteristic disregard for pomp and circumstance, was planning a world tour with his wife Charlotte Kerr instead!

By that time, some thirty-five years on, the details of *Der Besuch der alten Dame* must have been somewhat remote from Dürrenmatt's day-to-day thoughts, yet there is still a remarkable the degree of continuity between certain of his preoccupations even towards the end of his life and those concerns which seem to have been at the forefront of his mind in 1955 when he was writing the play. On 22nd November, 1990, Dürrenmatt delivered a speech in Zürich in honour of the President of Czechoslovakia, his fellow-playwright Václav Havel. As things turned out, it was to be Dürrenmatt's last public appearance in his native country. A lifelong dissident and outspoken critic of the brutal communist regime, Havel had been the obvious popular choice for leader following the break-up of that regime in late 1989, and was now in Switzerland to receive a prestigious award, the Gottlieb-Duttweiler-Preis, in recognition of his contribution to democracy. Dürrenmatt's chosen theme was freedom: the freedom which had been denied to Havel throughout so many years, and by contrast the freedom long enjoyed by every Swiss citizen. But, Dürrenmatt argued with characteristic wry humour, if Czechoslovakia before the collapse of the Iron Curtain had been a prison imposed on its citizens by the communist authorities, then Switzerland, despite its much-vaunted democracy, was also a prison, a different sort of prison admittedly, but one no less restrictive of individual freedom: in effect a self-imposed prison run on a voluntary basis by its very inmates. The Swiss, he observed, lock up their 'dissidents' too, the *Dienstverweigerer* or conscientious objectors who, in the view of some of the more reactionary citizens of Switzerland, pose such a threat to the armed neutrality of which they are so inordinately proud;[14] but any outsider can see that in reality the Swiss live their lives in exile, holed up in the fortress of that neutrality, cut off by choice from the rest of

14 Dürrenmatt's son, Peter, is a Protestant minister. His father was enormously proud of the fact that he once spent three months in gaol for refusing to do the National Service that is still compulsory for all Swiss men.

Europe. Neutrality suited Switzerland very well during the Second World War, and it still suits many Swiss even now, but neutrality should not be confused with freedom, and the idea that the Swiss are free is a delusion. Switzerland is

> ein Gefängnis, wohinein sich die Schweizer geflüchtet haben. Weil alles außerhalb des Gefängisses übereinander herfiel und weil sie nur im Gefängnis sicher sind, nicht überfallen zu werden, fühlen sich die Schweizer frei, freier als alle andern Menschen, frei als Gefangene im Gefängnis ihrer Neutralität. Es gibt nur eine Schwierigkeit für dieses Gefängnis, nämlich die, zu beweisen, daß es kein Gefängnis ist, sondern ein Hort der Freiheit, ist doch von außen gesehen ein Gefängnis ein Gefängnis und seine Insassen Gefangene, und wer gefangen ist, ist nicht frei.[15]

Before the collapse of the Iron Curtain, in countries like Czechoslovakia, the freedom of the individual was constantly under attack from doctrinaire totalitarianism, with its often bloodily enforced demands for absolute conformity. In today's ostensibly freer world, people everywhere are still constrained, but now almost entirely by economic factors: 'Die Politik hat sich auch bei uns aus der Ideologie in die Wirtschaft verzogen, ihre Fragen sind wirtschaftliche Fragen.' (*Kants Hoffnung*, 20) We are all in the hands of governments which, instead of leading, are able to do little more than react convulsively to the successive blows inflicted on them by the so-called free market economy. A world driven overwhelmingly by the desire to make money has no room for considerations such as respect for the rights or the dignity of others, nor for ethical scruples in matters of personal conduct. The individuals in our society, like the people of Güllen all those years ago, are motivated purely and simply by greed; and our society, in turn, is manipulated by financiers and currency speculators, just as Güllen was once manipulated by the richest woman in the world. So perhaps *Der Besuch der alten Dame* had not vanished from Dürrenmatt's mind in late 1990 after all. Güllen as a microcosm of Switzerland, the Gülleners as examples of the self-destructive force of greed, Claire Zachanassian as living proof of the corrosive power of great wealth. And above them all, Dürrenmatt's creature, Alfred Ill, asserting the dignity of the human spirit by accepting full responsibility for his actions so long ago. The people of Güllen surrender their dignity and their integrity in exchange for material gain; the Swiss, Dürrenmatt implies, do something very similar, for the point of their self-inflicted imprisonment is not, as they like to pretend to themselves, to safeguard their freedom–indeed far from

---

15 Dürrenmatt, 'Die Schweiz– ein Gefängnis,' *Kants Hoffnung* (Zürich, 1991), 15.

it–, but simply to preserve the source of their wealth: 'die Meinung [wird] immer stärker, der eigentliche Sinn des Gefängnisses liege nicht darin, die Freiheit der Gefangenen, sondern das Bankgeheimnis zu bewachen.' (17)

So in 1955, on the stage in the *Theatersaal* of the Golden Apostle in Güllen, the down-at-heel, inarticulate Alfred Ill showed his fellow-citizens how conscience can triumph over materialism; and in late 1990, in a world that had become more intensely materialistic with every intervening year, the ever-uncomfortable Fritz Dürrenmatt also mounted the stage, not far away from the theatre where that very play had first been performed, to remind his distinguished and no doubt wealthy audience, with a few deftly chosen words, that wealth and human dignity are uneasy bedfellows, and that freedom is not a matter of external barriers or political bluster, but a profoundly private thing of the spirit. He could hardly have picked a more appropriate subject for his final speech, or stage-managed a more appropriate setting for his final bow.

Suggestions for Further Reading

I PRIMARY

(A) COLLECTED EDITIONS OF DÜRRENMATT'S WORKS

Werkausgabe in dreißig Bänden (Zürich, 1980).

Gesammelte Werke in sieben Bänden ed. Franz Josef Görtz (Zürich, 1988).

(B) ANNOTATED EDITION OF *BESUCH DER ALTEN DAME*

Paul Kurt Ackermann (ed.) *Friedrich Dürrenmatt. Der Besuch der alten Dame* (London, 1957).

(C) INTERVIEWS WITH DÜRRENMATT

Heinz Ludwig Arnold *Friedrich Dürrenmatt. Gespräch mit Heinz Ludwig Arnold* (Zürich, 1976).

Siegfried Melchinger 'Wie schreibt man böse, wenn man gut lebt? Ein Gespräch mit Friedrich Dürrenmatt,' *Theater heute,* Vol. 9, No. 9, 1968, 6-8.

Kenneth S. Whitton 'Afternoon Conversation with an Uncomfortable Person, '*New German Studies,* Vol. 2, Spring 1974, 14-30.

II SECONDARY

Armin Arnold *Friedrich Dürrenmatt* (New York, 1972).

Hans Bänziger *Frisch und Dürrenmatt* (Bern, 1976[7]).

E.S. Dick	'Dürrenmatt's Der Besuch der alten Dame: Welttheater und Ritualspiel,' *Zeitschrift für deutsche Philologie*, Vol. 87, No. 4, October 1968, 498-509.
Heinrich Goertz	*Friedrich Dürrenmatt, mit Selbstzeugnissen und Bilddokumenten* (Reinbek bei Hamburg, 1987).
Urs Jenny	*Dürrenmatt. A Study of his Plays*, trans. by Keith Hamnett and Hugh Rorrison (London, 1978).
Jan Knopf	*Friedrich Dürrenmatt* (München, 1976).
Ulrich Profitlich	'Friedrich Dürrenmatt,' *Deutsche Dichter der Gegenwart. Ihr Leben und Werk*, hrsg. von Benno von Wiese (Berlin, 1973), 497-514.
Jürgen Söring & Jürg Flury (Hrsg.)	*Hommage à Friedrich Dürrenmatt* (Frankfurt am Main, 1991).
Timo Tuisanen	*Dürrenmatt. A Study in Plays, Prose, Theory* (Princeton, 1977).
Kenneth S. Whitton	*Dürrenmatt: Reinterpretation in Retrospect* (Oxford, Hamburg & New York, 1990).